Suzhou Creek

SHANGHAI

China Guides Series Limited

China Guides Series Limited
P O Box 31395 Causeway Bay
Hong Kong

Text by Jill Hunt; Shann Davies; Lynn M. Osen and Ian Findlay
Revised by Ian Findlay
Introductions by David Bonavia and Richard Hughes
Photographs by Magnus Bartlett and pictures of the Jinjiang Club
by Ellen Rudolph

Contents

Shanghai Mansions

Shanghai Yesterday and Today

An introduction to Shanghai by David Bonavia

Shanghai — with a population estimated at some 11 million — is the biggest city in China. Exact census figures are not available, but the only other city in the world with a comparable population is Tokyo.

Shanghai is also one of the world's youngest cities, having been built mainly in the second half of the 19th century and the first half of the 20th. But in architectural terms it is the least Chinese city in China.

In 1832, when the first westerners set foot in Shanghai, it was a walled city of less than 300,000 people, thriving off the trade between the coast and the provinces on the middle and upper reaches of the Yangtse River (nowadays called Changjiang or 'Long River').

In that year the British East India Company dispatched a warship from Canton, the big southern city which was the only place where foreigners were allowed to reside and trade under the isolationist policy of the Qing (Ch'ing) or Manchu Dynasty. A British landing party went ashore and literally broke down the door of the local magistracy to demand an interview, while at the same time distributing Chinese-language pamphlets to the local people explaining the benefits of international trade.

The local authorities stubbornly refused to permit the opening of Shanghai as a trading port, fearing that insidious foreign influences would undermine the local economy and society. In 1842, during the First Opium War, a British fleet bombarded the fortifications and routed the garrison. As part of the Treaty of Nanking which ended the war, western merchants were granted permission to trade and lease land on the west bank of the Huangpu River.

In 1853-54, the foreign settlement became a refuge for hundreds of thousands of Chinese people from the surrounding area, who were fleeing from the fighting between the imperial troops and the rebel army of the Taipings — a pseudo-Christian sect which nearly succeeded in overthrowing the Manchu Dynasty.

The combination of a good port, western technology and commerce, and a limitless local work-force soon made Shanghai one of the leading trading centres in the East, and grandiose stone buildings were put up along the central waterfront, or Bund, to house the great banks, trading houses and consulates of the day.

The city was divided into the British-dominated International Settlement, the French Concession (where there were in fact relatively few French people), the Chinese City to the south and the large Chinese suburb of Zhabei on the bank of Suzhou Creek to the north of the main city. The United States and many European countries had consulates and were represented on the Municipal Council, and prosperous traders built fine houses for themselves in the western style. The luxury hotels are impressive still today, with their gaudy art déco interiors and huge bathrooms.

As a self-governing city not under the authority of the central government in Peking, Shanghai attracted every kind of fortune-hunter, rebel, conspirator and smuggler. It became known as the 'paradise of adventurers', and was famed throughout the world for its luxurious and flamboyant life-style. Every form of vice flourished. The city's name entered the English languages as a verb meaning 'to kidnap'.

Great industries were founded — particularly for the manufacture of textiles — and many Chinese merchants became modern industrialists, bankers and millionaires. But the living standards for most of the Chinese people were poor and squalid, and they were treated with contempt by most of the foreigners. The resentment which this bred — as well as the city's role as a sanctuary from the authority of the Chinese government — made Shanghai a hotbed of revolutionaries and anarchists. The Chinese Communist Party was founded there in 1921, and an influential left-wing movement sprang up among the city's Chinese intellectuals.

After the founding of the People's Republic of China in 1949, the Communist Party mounted a determined effort to turn Shanghai from a symbol of national humiliation into a token of China's dreams and ambitions. Crime and prostitution rings were broken up; wealthy industrialists were encouraged to stay on and manage their factories until such time as they would be taken over by the State. The city became the new regime's biggest port and most important trading and manufacturing centre.

Shanghai's industry has continued to grow and develop, and the city now exports numerous products including machine tools, textiles, arts and crafts and light industrial consumer goods. Shanghai people — speaking their distinctive dialect — are known throughout China as astute businessmen well versed in the ways of world commerce.

The city trades with some 20,000 firms in 150 countries. In addition, it has industries serving the domestic market, making iron and steel, petrochemicals, ships, transistors and TV sets, chemical fibres, watches, sewing machines, bicycles, cars and trucks, pharmaceutical products, medical equipment and measuring instruments.

Through its links with central and western China via the Yangtse River, Shanghai is the most important supplier of industrial equipment and consumer goods to those areas, and the biggest

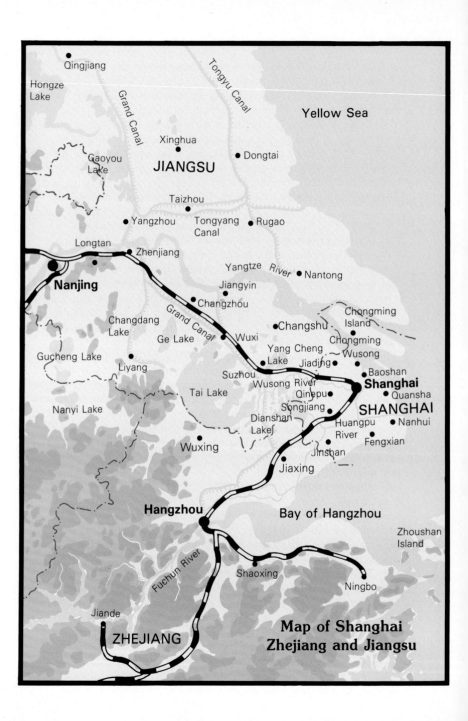

Map of Shanghai
Zhejiang and Jiangsu

商品果業

Pre-1949 architecture

market for their produce. Vessels from every significant shipping company in the world throng its extensive port. It is also an aviation centre, with a direct link to Japan, and it is connected by rail to all the major economic regions of China.

With its western-style buildings and its memories of the foreign settlement, Shanghai has a cosmopolitanly-minded population, and is always in the forefront of any new trends in fashion and design. It has an elaborate and lavish cuisine in which the colour and presentation of food is taken almost as seriously as its flavour.

The city's Fudan (New Dawn) University is one of the country's biggest, and nowadays accepts foreign as well as Chinese students. Shanghai has pioneered experiments in worker-education by sending people from the shop floor to advanced technical colleges to improve their theoretical knowledge and skills. The city has numerous technical design institutes.

Many of the impressive advances in Chinese medicine have stemmed from Shanghai, with its large and relatively well-equipped hospitals, where surgeons can re-attach severed limbs and carry out complex operations with no anaesthetics other than acupuncture.

Although housing and public amenities are under severe strain from the huge population, and great improvements in living standards are needed, Shanghai stands in the forefront of China's drive to modernize her industry, agriculture, science, technology and defence. Its past links with the outside world are being turned to good use in the new outward-looking policy of trade and technological exchange with other countries.

*David Bonavia is the China correspondent of **The Times** of London and of the Hong Kong-based **Far Eastern Economic Review**.*

Shanghai Recalled

By Richard Hughes

It is impossible for the visitor to spend a dull day in Shanghai. I lived there in 1940, made regular visits when I was based in Peking as a reporter in 1956-57, and made another brief return after the passage of a further 16 years in 1973.

There have of course been many changes in life and living. For the locals, it is a far better city. Gone today are the 1940 battalions of deformed and diseased beggars and the armies of child street-walkers. Gone are the terrible factories of forced child-labour. Gone are the hundreds of frozen corpses in the backalleys each winter.

The ghosts of the western traders have been driven out of the old Shanghai Club by a huge Buddha-like statue of the late Chairman Mao. The Club, now called the Dongfeng (East Wind), serves as a stopover hostelry for Chinese travellers. My old memories ached to discover that the celebrated Long Bar (110 feet) had been divided into three sections, over which icecream and peanuts were available for non-member children and women, previously banned from the premises. The once sacrosanct smoking room, opposite the Long Bar, where honourable members dozed after a heavy tiffin draped under copies of *The Times* from London, is now a communal overnight dormitory, with rolled mattresses and dangling underwear.

The old Cathay Hotel is now the Peace Hotel. The old racecourse — already a park and a People's Square in 1956 — is the roof of the largest and deepest air-raid shelter in Shanghai, following underground the winding course of the city's most famous shopping street, Nanjing Road. Broadway Mansions — now Shanghai Mansions — has the most efficient elevator service in China; from its lofty roof, one can salute furtively the ancient abandoned British Consulate.

Not even veteran Party cadres could recall the sinister names of Delmonte's or Farren's — former gambling casinos, now schools for dramatic and theatrical training. 'Do you remember "Demon" Hyde, the tough San Francisco boss of Delmonte's in the forties?' No-one does . . .

Laundry hangs in public from the verandahs of millionaire residences which have survived along the former Avenue Joffre in the old French Concession — now converted into worker's tenements.

The street once called 'Blood Alley' is eminently respectable now; once it was a notorious street-walkers' beat.

The old French Club was 'closed for repairs' when I squinted at it in 1973, but now has been reopened as the Jinjiang Club, with an indoor swimming pool, bowling alley and billiard rooms, a huge ballroom, and high-class French cuisine in the restaurant. It is intended primarily to cater for tourists but local people come for dinner and evening swimming. They can even play mahjong there — forbidden elsewhere in China.

One of my favourite eating places in Shanghai was the Xinya Restaurant in Nanjing Road. I used to go there regularly. The name in English has been removed from the door, but I had not forgotten the number — 719.

There was, I thought, little change inside the crowded two floors of the restaurant. The same diners — mostly family groups — were still eating noisily, gaily, comfortably, abundantly. The same stout barman — it seemed to me — was pouring the same lively Tsingtao beer into the same glass mugs. And there was the same rich enduring fragrance of good Chinese cooking.

'The food is the same,' I was assured by an old waiter, who unbelievably remembered me after 16 years. He eyed me sharply when I asked for a whisky. He brought me a half empty bottle of White Horse, and with difficulty prised open its long-sealed and semi-embalmed stopper.

'This will cost you more than the dinner,' he warned me, lifting the familiar silver egg-cup measure. 'We don't get any more whisky now. The price is fixed.'

He was right. The dinner — luscious prawns, bird's nest soup and tender beef with oyster sauce — cost me maybe US$1. The two straight whiskies cost more than US$2. Just before I left, my friend looked swiftly around, then, interposing his body between my cubicle and the cashier, poured me a third whisky — on the honourable house! We smiled together.

You can't tip waiters in China now. But he could tip me — in Shanghai. There's no place like it.

Journalist Richard Hughes, now immortalized as Craw in Le Carré's bestseller **The Honourable Schoolboy,** *left his native Australia for Asia in 1940. One of the best-known pressmen in the Far East, his career as a correspondent spans over forty years. He is the author of* **Hong Kong: Borrowed Place — Borrowed Time** *and* **Foreign Devil: Thirty Years of Reporting in the Far East.** *Since 1957 Richard Hughes has lived in Hong Kong, where he continues to write for newspapers and periodicals.*

Policeman and fireman

Getting to Shanghai

Direct routes Both the Chinese airline, CAAC (Civil Aviation Administration of China) and Japan Air Lines, operate regular flights between Shanghai and Tokyo via Osaka. Flying time to Tokyo from Shanghai is four hours. Cathay Pacific have a direct service from Hong Kong and Pan American at present operate a service out of Shanghai to Tokyo and New York.

A Chinese passenger ship, the *Shanghai*, sails between Hong Kong and Shanghai twice a month. The ship, which can accommodate over 400 passengers in its five classes, has a swimming pool, ballroom, cinema, shops, clinic, and restaurants serving both Chinese and western food. The voyage takes around 58 hours. Shanghai is also one of the main ports of call of various tourist cruise ships.

Via Canton One of the routes most frequently used by foreign visitors to Shanghai is from Hong Kong via Canton. There are a variety of different means of travelling from Hong Kong to the southern Chinese city of Canton — by air on CAAC flights, by train, by hovercraft, or even passenger liner. From Canton there are regular domestic CAAC flights up to Shanghai, taking two hours. There are also two express trains a day. The journey takes around 33 hours, but 'soft' class accommodation on China's engagingly old-fashioned express trains is usually well-equipped and comfortable.

Via Peking A number of international airlines already fly to Peking — including Japan Air Lines and some of the major European carriers. From Peking there are two daily express trains to Shanghai, taking around 20 hours, and regular CAAC flights, which take just under two hours.

Passengers on CAAC are warned that the airline levies charges of up to 25% of the value of the ticket for late cancellation and no-show.

Hotels

In Shanghai, as in other cities in China open to foreigners, tourists travelling in groups do not choose the hotel they stay in, but are allocated a hotel by CITS (China International Travel Service). Visitors travelling independently may try and request to stay in a particular hotel, although, with the ever-increasing number of visitors, Shanghai's hotel facilities are often stretched to their limits, and such requests may not be successful.

Shanghai's hotels are undoubtedly amongst the best in China. Mostly built in the 1920s and '30s, when Shanghai, the 'Paris of the East', was the most sophisticated destination for international travellers, the hotels have managed to retain something of the opulence of that era. The art déco mood of the large public areas, the high ceilings, the chandeliers, the wooden-panelled walls, and comfortably old-fashioned rooms, give Shanghai's hotels a special quality.

Rooms are invariably warm in winter and most are now air-conditioned in summer. Bathrooms are usually large, with big baths and aging showers, but unlike some of their more modern equivalents in China, everything works. There are outlets for electric razors but sometimes designed for old-style plugs. The current is 220 volts.

Service, especially from some of the older members of staff who learnt their excellent English and French in the days before 1949, is usually very good. On each floor there is a service desk manned by staff who supply rooms with flasks of hot and cold water and towels. They also collect and deliver laundry, keep room keys, place international telephone calls, and provide ice, beer or soft drinks. Thefts from hotel rooms are almost unheard of, but it is best not to leave doors unlocked or valuables clearly visible.

All hotels have post office and money changing facilities. Most have small shops selling souvenirs, tourist maps and guides, as well as imported liquor and film.

笼柏饭店　虹桥路2419号

Cypress Hotel (Longbo Hotel) 2419 Hongqiao Road. This is the first hotel designed for foreign tourists to be completed in Shanghai since the rapid expansion of China's tourist industry in 1978. It opened in the summer of 1982. The highrise block, with 162 rooms, is set in spacious grounds in the western suburbs of the city, near the airport. Although the hotel is comfortable and has good facilities, it lacks the character of Shanghai's older hotels.

Interiors, Peace Hotel

达华宾馆　延安西路914号
Dahua Guesthouse 914 Yan'an Road West tel. 523079.
Originally an apartment block, this nine-storey building dates from
1937. The hotel has comfortable rooms and pleasant service, but
suffers from being in the west of the city and rather far from the
central shopping area. With no garden, it is set directly on the street,
and tends to be rather noisy.

衡山宾馆　衡山路534号
Hengshan Hotel 534 Hengshan Road tel. 377050. This 15-storey
hotel is another converted apartment block, previously called the
Picardie. Extensive renovation in the latter part of 1979 has greatly
improved facilities. Situated in the southwest of the city, the hotel is
far away from the centre of Shanghai.

锦江饭店　长乐路189号
Jinjiang Hotel 189 Changle Road tel. 534242. In the heart of the
old French quarter, this elegant hotel set in a large garden was
originally a private hotel for French residents in Shanghai. Now, with
three new buildings added, it is the largest of the city's hotels, with
over 800 rooms. It has particularly good services, with a large telex
room, a well-stocked bookshop and souvenir shop, two coffee
shops, and men's and women's hairdressers. It is within easy walking
distance of Nanjing Road.

　　The hotel's oldest building, the north block, with its grand
curving steps leading up to the columned entrance, dates from
1931. Inside, the wooden-panelled rooms are quietly comfortable,
and the elevators have an old-world charm reminiscent of pre-war
Europe. The palatial dining rooms on the upper floors, serving both
Chinese and western food, are magnificent settings for banquets.

　　It was here at the Jinjiang Hotel that Premier Chou En-lai and
President Nixon completed the historic Shanghai Communiqué in
February 1972, opening up the way for the future development of
relations between the United States and China.

静安宾馆　华山路370号
Jingan Guesthouse 370 Huashan Road tel. 563050. Formerly a
smart private hotel for foreign residents, this quiet and comfortable
guesthouse offers excellent service and particularly good food —
both Chinese and western. Set in a pleasant garden, it is near
Nanjing Road West, but not within walking distance of the waterfront
and the main shopping area.

新亚饭店　天潼路422号
New Asia Hotel 422 Tiantong Road tel. 242210. First opened in

1934, the New Asia Hotel was one of Shanghai's most famous
establishments. It is centrally located on the corner of Tiantong Road
and Sichuan Road North. Opposite the hotel is the Central Post
Office and behind the Post Office lies the Suzhou Creek which is
always bustling with acitivity. There are over 300 rooms in this eight-
storey hotel. On the ground floor a spacious restaurant serves
inexpensive but good Canton, Shanghai, and Sichuan food.

华侨饭店　南京西路104号
Overseas Chinese Hotel 104 Nanjing Road West tel. 226226. The
hotel, which is just to the east of the Park Hotel, is very centrally
situated. As its name suggests, it has been used almost entirely for
Overseas Chinese visitors.

国际饭店　南京西路170号
Park Hotel 170 Nanjing Road West tel. 225225. Until recently
called the International, or Guoji, Hotel, this hotel has now reverted
to its pre-1949 name. With 24 storeys, it is the tallest building in
Shanghai. Built in 1934, with an excellent location overlooking the
racecourse (now Renmin Park), the Park Hotel was well known for
its famous chefs and its fashionable daily tea dance.

There are very few reminders today of the hotel's past other
than its excellent restaurant. Until recently the hotel was used almost
entirely for Overseas Chinese and for compatriots (Chinese visitors
from Hong Kong and Macau).

和平饭店北楼　南京东路20号
Peace Hotel 20 Nanjing Road East tel. 211244. Built in 1928 and
formerly known as the Cathay, this famous 11-storey landmark, with
its distinctive green-roofed tower, stands at the north corner of
Nanjing Road and the waterfront. The former Palace Hotel, opposite
on the south side of Nanjing Road, which dates from 1906, has now
been incorporated to form a smaller south wing of the Peace Hotel.

This was the most magnificent of the pre-1949 hotels, and
everyone of note who visited Shanghai stayed at the Cathay, or, at
least, was seen dancing at the hotel's roof-top Tower Restaurant.
Now, although rather threadbare in places, reminders of the hotel's
past remain in the softly-lit lobby, with its revolving doors, art déco
windows and lamp stands, and in the ornate, heavily decorated
dining room on the eighth floor which overlooks the waterfront and
the river.

Both wings have dining rooms, with impressive Chinese and
western menus, and elegant banquets are served in the banqueting
rooms on the upper floors of the north wing. A first-floor café serves
cakes and ice-cream, and both imported and local alcohol from mid-

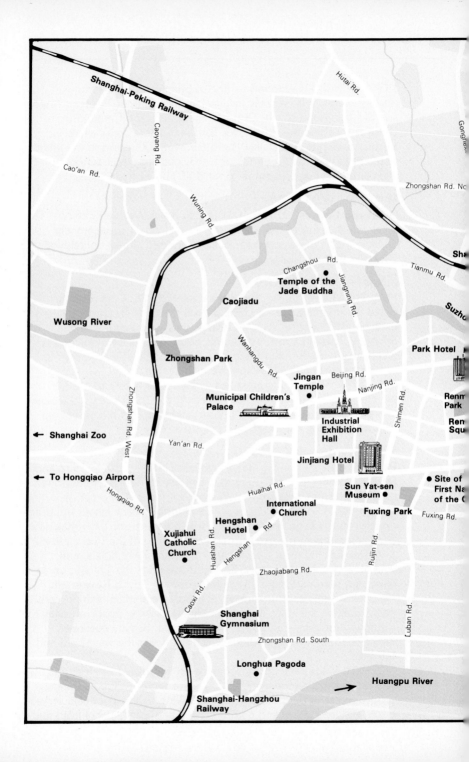

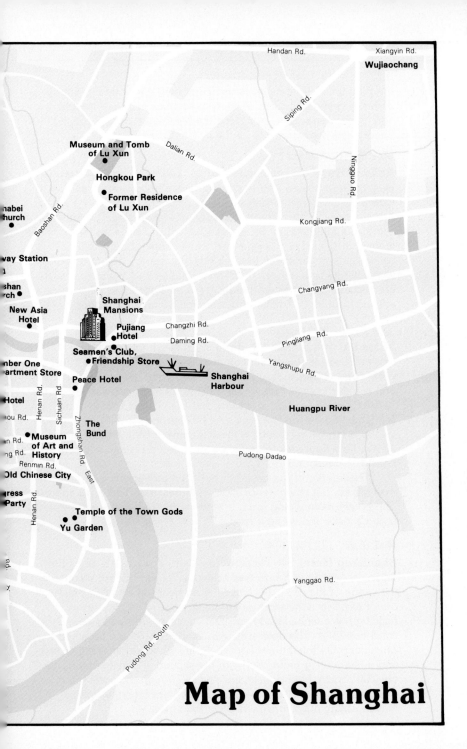

Handan Rd.

Xiangyin Rd.

Wujiaochang

Siping Rd.

**Museum and Tomb
of Lu Xun**

Dalian Rd.

Hongkou Park

Ningguo Rd.

**Former Residence
of Lu Xun**

nabei
hurch

Baoshan Rd.

Kongjiang Rd.

vay Station

shan
rch

Changyang Rd.

**New Asia
Hotel**

**Shanghai
Mansions**

Changzhi Rd.

**Pujiang
Hotel**

Daming Rd.

Pingliang Rd.

**Seamen's Club,
Friendship Store**

Yangshupu Rd.

nber One
artment Store

Peace Hotel

**Shanghai
Harbour**

Henan Rd.

Sichuan Rd.

Hotel

ou Rd.

Huangpu River

Zhongshan Rd. East

**The
Bund**

n Rd.

**Museum
of Art and
History**

Pudong Dadao

ng Rd.

Renmin Rd.

Old Chinese City

Henan Rd.

ress
Party

Temple of the Town Gods

Yu Garden

Yanggao Rd.

Rd.

y.

Pudong Rd. South

Map of Shanghai

morning until late at night. A service desk in the lobby helps book day-trips to nearby places of interest, such as Suzhou, Hangzhou and Wuxi. It may be worth trying the hairdresser here — Shanghai's hairdressers are reputed to be the best in China.

浦江饭店　黄浦路17号
Pujiang Hotel 17 Huangpu Road tel. 246388. Formerly the elegant Astor House, this slightly run-down hotel is set in an extremely convenient location, just one minute from Shanghai Mansions on Sichuan Road North. On the other side of the street stands the International Seaman's Club which overlooks the Huangpu River. For foreigners on a low budget the Pujiang has become a popular cheap hotel. It offers dormitory accommodation with eight beds to a room. Each room has its own bathroom. With easy access to the centre of the city it is ideal for those who are passing through Shanghai with little time for much exploring.

上海大厦　北苏州路20号
Shanghai Mansions 20 Suzhou Road North tel. 244186. This typical '30s-style skyscraper commands a magnificent view from the north bank of the Suzhou Creek, looking down along the waterfront and across the city of Shanghai. Built in 1934, Broadway Mansions, as the 22-storey red-brick building was then called, was a smart residential hotel, which at one time housed the US Military Advisory Group on the lower floors, with apartments for the foreign press above. One floor was set aside for the bar and restaurant of the Foreign Correspondents' Club of China.

The interior of the hotel has not been particularly well maintained, but recent renovation work has improved some rooms. The hotel's main dining room is now on the third floor, and serves both Chinese and western food.

申江饭店　汉口路740号
Shenjiang Hotel 740 Hankou Road tel. 225115. This small hotel, originally called the Yanzi, was built in 1934. It is ideally situated in the centre of the city but is tucked away near the People's Square out of earshot of the worst of the traffic noise. The nine-storey building has a white facade and French-style windows leading on to small balconies. The hotel was renovated in 1978 and renamed Shenjiang. On the ground floor there are shops, four dining rooms and a banqueting room. Between the second and eighth floors there are 200 rooms, both double and single. Though the hotel caters mainly for Overseas Chinese and visitors from Hong Kong and Macau, many other foreigners have lived here.

西郊宾馆　虹桥路1921号

Western Suburbs Guesthouse 1921 Hongqiao Road tel. 379643.
Set in more than 170 hectares of beautifully kept grounds, this is a
secluded, luxurious, and very expensive guesthouse, used mainly by
official delegations, foreign companies and some upmarket tour
groups. The guesthouse complex consists of seven buildings; some
were built pre-1949 as private houses, others were put up in the
1950s, and the latest addition was completed in 1981. Building
Number Four, originally the private house of a wealthy businessman,
has a swimming pool, a disco, and magnificent garden room, now
used as a lounge. The guesthouse is about 10 minutes by taxi from
the airport and 20 minutes from the city centre.

兴国宾馆　兴国路72号

Xingguo Guesthouse 72 Xingguo Road tel. 374503. This
exclusive guesthouse has no sign on its door and there is no other
indication of what could be behind its facade. It lies off Huaihai
Middle Road about eight blocks from the Jinjiang Hotel. Most taxi
drivers do not know the guesthouse so if you want to visit make
sure you give careful directions.

The guesthouse complex consists of a number of spacious
private houses built before the Second World War. The gardens are
well looked after and there is a peace about the place which one
does not get in some of the centrally located hotels.

The guesthouse is not for the poor traveller and is more often
used for special travel groups, businessmen or foreign companies.
To rent one of the houses will cost over US$600 per day, but one
can rent a room in one of the smaller houses for US$45–US$65
per day. Each house is kept extremely clean and the staff are
attentive. The house staff also do the cooking but they only produce
Chinese food. For those who desperately want a western meal it is
just a short stroll to the Jinjiang Hotel.

There are several other guesthouses in Shanghai similar in quality
and price to the Western Suburbs Guesthouse and the Xingguo
Guesthouse:

东湖宾馆　新乐路167号
Donghu Guesthouse 167 Xinyue Road tel. 370050

虹桥宾馆　虹桥路159号
Hongqiao Guesthouse 159 Hongqiao Road tel. 372170

瑞金宾馆　瑞金路118号
Ruijin Guesthouse 118 Ruijin Road tel. 372653

For advance booking for these guesthouses telephone 374861/378222.

Clubs

International Club 63 Yan'an Road West tel. 538455. If one
wishes to shun the opulent art déco world of the Jinjiang Club then
the International is ideal. Much smaller than its well-known counter-
part, there are two tennis courts and a small swimming pool, and for
those who like team games there are basketball courts. Hours at the
club vary so it is best to call before going. There is also a theatre here
which puts on the occasional play or film.

Jinjiang Club 58 Maoming Road tel. 375334. Deep in the old
French Concession the former Cercle Sportif, dating from 1921, is
an ideal place to spend a quiet day away from the rigours of travelling
or sightseeing. Open seven days a weeks the club offers a variety of
entertainment at very reasonable prices. For the energetic there is
tennis on well-kept clay courts (8 am – 6 pm), table tennis (11 am –
11 pm), and bowling (11 am – 11 pm). For those who wish to take
things a little easier there is a 175-foot swimming pool (9 am –
10.30 pm; trunks and towels can be hired) and snooker on the best
tables in Shanghai (11 am – 11 pm). There is a games room
(11 am – 11 pm) with various electronic games machines and pin-ball
machines, and also facilities for chess and mahjong.

Climate and Clothing

Shanghai experiences extremes of climate. Winters are cold with
temperatures dipping below freezing and there are occasional
snowfalls. Summer is very hot with daytime highs often reaching the
upper 90s, although this is not always too uncomfortable thanks to
constant breezes off the river and airconditioning in most hotels. On
average there are 11 days of rain in the summer months.

Spring usually has warm days with cool nights and there are
occasional showers. Autumn is by far the best time to visit the city.
The average temperature is 75°F (24°C) during the day and 56°F
(14°C) at night and the skies are as clear as the industrial haze
will permit.

Compared to other Chinese cities Shanghai is chic but the same
dress rules for foreigners apply as elsewhere. Men need not wear ties
and jackets, women should avoid revealing garb and everyone
should have comfortable shoes. Formal dress is never required
although it is acceptable to wear a cocktail dress at official banquets.

Getting around Shanghai

Shanghai is a vast city, but the fairly regular pattern of the central area, with the main streets crossing at right angles, together with the variety of landmarks, makes it a relatively easy city to get around. Zhongshan Road East, or the Bund as it used to be called, and Nanjing Road, where many of the best shops and restaurants can be found, will be easily remembered focal points for any visitor to Shanghai, however short the stay.

Taxis are not found cruising the streets. They should be ordered from hotel service desks or by telephoning the hotels. Fares are not expensive, and it is worth keeping the same taxi until a sightseeing or shopping expedition is finished. Tipping is not allowed.

There are 152 colour-coded bus and trolleybus lines in the city. Some of them run throughout the night. Fares are only a few *fen*, but buses are invariably crowded, and even a Chinese-speaking visitor will find it difficult to convey the correct fare to the conductor, or be confident of being let off at the destination.

For short trips it is possible to take a motorized trishaw but again, because the drivers are not used to foreign passengers, it may be difficult to explain exactly where you want to go.

Food and Drink

Shanghai has over 600 restaurants, which can cook more than 2000 different Chinese dishes. Traditionally the most cosmopolitan of all Chinese cities, it is not surprising that Shanghai's restaurants offer many different types of cuisine — Sichuan, Canton, Peking, Suzhou, Moslem, and even a few restaurants with an entirely European menu. The people of Shanghai delight in eating out, and, since the demand for tables invariably exceeds the supply, it is essential for a large group to make reservations. Many places close their kitchens around 7.30pm and it is worth being punctual, especially when ordering Shanghai food which can often take up to half an hour to prepare.

Shanghai dishes should be eaten very hot, as soon as they arrive on the table. This is because the local cuisine uses a lot of oil which makes a dish taste heavy if it is left to get cold. On the other hand, some well-known cold dishes are particularly identified with Shanghai — drunken chicken, smoked fish, vegetarian 'goose'. Shanghai cooking makes use of the best of freshwater and sea fish — eel, carp, shrimps, and, most celebrated of all, the Shanghai freshwater crabs, in season from October to December — together with an abundance of fresh local vegetables and fruit. Noodles and steamed dumplings are eaten as well as rice. Dishes may be braised, steamed, fried in batter, or marinated and grilled. Ginger, sugar, *shaoxing* wine, and soy, are used extensively in sauces. Some of the best soups are substantial dishes made up of meat, vegetables, and transparent rice vermicelli.

Shanghai's cuisine has always been noted for its elegant presentation, and dishes served at banquets are as much a delight to the eye as to the stomach. Particularly spectacular are the hors-d'oeuvres of cold vegetables and meats, ingeniously arranged to resemble exotic birds or flowers.

The people of Shanghai are very fond of snacks, and innumerable small restaurants and coffee shops serve a variety of sweet and savoury snacks, either to be taken away, or devoured on the spot (see page 40). Favourite snacks include steamed dumplings filled with minced pork, round sesame cakes, steamed rice-flour dough stuffed with nuts and sweetened sesame seed, fried beef dumplings, onion pastries, and eight-jewelled rice, which is glutinous rice topped with bits of dried fruit, sugar and nuts.

Pastries and cakes are also highly popular, and anyone with a sweet tooth will find it hard to walk past the many cake shops in

The Red House

Nanjing Road, their windows packed with a range of plain buns, pastries stuffed with cream, and ornately decorated cakes in many shades of pastel icing.

Restaurants which cater to foreigners, such as some of those in the following list, reserve special areas for their foreign clientele, but visitors, especially if their group is small, can insist on eating with the locals. The quantity of food served to foreigners who book meals in local restaurants can sometimes be rather overwhelming — a banquet often has as many as 15 courses. One way to ensure a smaller meal is to specify the number of courses when the reservation is being made, and to ask for a low price per head. Prices for a banquet usually range from 20-50 yuan a head, depending on the restaurant. Prices for the Chinese are considerably lower.

As in other Chinese cities, no imported liquor is served in the restaurants, although it can be bought in many hotel shops. Shanghai beer is cheap and good, and Chinese vodka is also palatable. The local brandy is not unlike a rough Mediterranean brandy, but Chinese whisky and gin in no way resemble their European counter-

Breakfast, Peace Hotel

parts. Amongst Chinese wines and spirits the best known are the
very potent clear spirits made from sorghum, such as *maotai*, and
the less strong glutinous rice yellow wine, *shaoxing*, some kinds of
which are served warm. The Chinese produce various red and white
grape wines. Although these are mostly rather sweet, a new dry
Chinese white and red wine is becoming increasingly available.
Chinese soft drinks are usually very sweet, and tea makes a better
drink after a large meal.

For unusual drinks, there can be little in Shanghai to beat the
Chinese liquor cocktails created by an imaginative barman at the
Peace Hotel — the Panda (*maotai*, raw egg, and sugar), the Shanghai
(gin and white wine) and the Peace (whisky and sherry).

Recommended Restaurants

Canton

美心　陕西南路 314 号
Meixin 314 Shaanxi Road South tel. 373919. This is a large and
popular Cantonese restaurant, but, as with all Cantonese food in
Shanghai, the cooking has adopted something of a Shanghai
approach, particularly in its use of oil. The fried rice here is a
particular speciality — it is almost a meal in itself, packed with an
enormous variety of meats, vegetables and fish.

新雅　南京东路 719 号
Xinya 719 Nanjing Road East tel. 224393. This comfortable
restaurant serving Cantonese-style food has long been a favourite,
both with foreigners and with the Chinese. Like many of the restaurants in Nanjing Road, the first floor is a busy cake and pastry shop,
and the dining tables are on the second and third floors. Some of
the old waiters in the quiet wooden-panelled dining rooms on the
third floor have worked there since before 1949, and speak excellent
English. The service is, understandably, impeccable, and the food of
high quality. Reservations need to be made several days in advance.

Moslem

清真饭店　福州路 710 号
Qingzhen Fandian 710 Fuzhou Road tel. 224787. Situated
centrally, this friendly Moslem restaurant is one of the best in
Shanghai and is highly recommended. Besides the standard Moslem
dishes, the restaurant serves some dishes from Xinjiang in northwest
China.

Ningbo

宁波饭店　西藏中路 162 号

Ningbo Fandian 162 Xizang Middle Road tel. 225280. A short walk from the Park Hotel, this is one of the best-known restaurants specializing in food from Ningbo, the major sea-port in northern Zhejiang Province. The Ningbo Fandian has been in business since 1937 and the chefs are very proud of their work. Worth trying here are the fish dishes, the braised meat, and the shrimps.

Peking

北京饭店　霍山路 68 号

Beijing Fandian 68 Huoshan Road tel. 451151. This is without doubt one of the best Peking restaurants in town. It does not have the style of some of Shanghai's better-known restaurants and is a little out of the way for many visitors, situated five blocks northeast of the Shanghai – Hong Kong Pier. But for those interested in visiting an old part of the city which few foreigners ever get to see the trip is worth it. It is an ideal place for those on a low budget. Chicken and duck dishes are specially recommended.

Shandong

首都饭庄　人民路 60 号

Shoudu Fanzhuang 60 Renmin Road tel. 554581. Food from the northern province of Shandong — the province lying between Jiangsu and Peking — is served here. Although some find Shandong cuisine rather sweet and sometimes heavy, banquets held in this restaurant have always been popular with foreign visitors. A speciality worth trying is their fish, chicken and bamboo dish, cooked in wine.

Shanghai

东风饭店　中山东一路 3 号

Dongfeng Hotel 3 Zhongshan Number One Road East tel. 218060. The restaurant in this hotel for Chinese is worth visiting if only to see the Long Bar — once the most famous bar in the East. Over a hundred feet long, the bar was the focal point of the prestigious men-only Shanghai Club. Before 1949 a visit to Shanghai was not complete without a drink being bought by a member of this British-style club. Now, instead of pink gins, a variety of Shanghai dishes are served from what was reputedly the longest bar in the world.

老正兴　九江路 566 号
Old Prosperity (Laozhengxing) 566 Jiujiang Road tel. 293153. This is another long-established eating place serving traditional Shanghai food, and specializing in freshwater fish, crabs, and turtles. In a narrow street off Nanjing Road East, this small restaurant is housed in a two-storey old-style building, and has apparently not been used to catering to many foreign visitors recently.

上海老饭店　福佑路 242 号
Old Town Restaurant (Lao Fandian) 242 Fuyou Road tel. 282782. Set in the old Chinese City near the Yu Garden, this famous old restaurant is generally thought to serve the most authentic Shanghai food in the city. Everyday dishes served in the ordinary section of the restaurant are excellent, and banquets can be superb, offering a chance to experience some of the best of the city's traditional cuisine — shrimps sautéed with egg white, carp in a rich tomato sauce, a crisp roast duck, Shanghai-style, a soup of sliced salted pork, chicken and bamboo shoots, and some perfect samples of Shanghai's savoury pastries and steamed dumplings. The restaurant makes an ideal lunch place after a visit to the Yu Garden. For important occasions it has even been possible to arrange for the restaurant to provide a special banquet in the Yu Garden itself.

杨州饭店　南京东路 308 号
Yangzhou Fandian 308 Nanjing Road East tel. 222779. One of the city's most popular restaurants, the Yangzhou serves some of the best Shanghai food to be had anywhere. Their wide menu ranges from simple but excellent dishes including many varieties of dumplings, noodles, and beancurd specialities, to wild duck — a rarity in Shanghai's restaurants. Banquets here can always be relied upon to be excellent. Since the restaurant always seems to be packed, reservations should be made well in advance.

Sichuan

绿杨村　南京东路 763 号
Luyangcun 763 Nanjing Road East tel. 737221. Downstairs during the day snacks are served, but upstairs, the restaurant provides some interesting dishes from nearby Jiangsu Province and also from Sichuan. Try the Jiangsu fried duck or tender chicken breasts, wrapped in paper, then fried in oil. Originally opened in 1931, the restaurant has long experience in catering to locals and foreign visitors.

桂花赤豆地力

甜美

Food stall, Nanjing Road

梅龙镇酒家　南京西路 1081 弄 22 号
Meilongzhen Jiujia 1081 Nanjing Road West, 22 Long tel. 535353.
Of the restaurants in Shanghai which specialize in Sichuan cooking
the Meilongzhen is one of the best. This restaurant first opened in 1938
on Weihaiwei Road and moved to Nanjing Road in the 1950s. In
1978 the whole restaurant was renovated and redesigned. There are
now more than 200 items on the menu with a few which are special
to the Meilongzhen. Among the best of these are their chicken soup
and crisp chicken. Vegetables here are usually excellent and so is the
beancurd, particularly the Longyuan beancurd.

新亚饭店　天潼路 422 号
New Asia Hotel 422 Tiantong Road tel. 242210. Across the road
from the Central Post Office, the New Asia Hotel's ground floor
restaurant serves a variety of regional dishes but by far the best are
its Sichuan dishes. It is reasonably priced and a good alternative to
the more expensive hotels such as the Peace and the Jinjiang.

四川饭店　南京东路 457 号
Sichuan Fandian 457 Nanjing Road East tel. 221965. It is
sometimes said that the best Sichuan food in China is to be found in
Peking and Shanghai. As this restaurant is considered one of the best
Sichuan eating places in Shanghai, it is certainly worth a visit. Any of
the typical Sichuan dishes strongly spiced with garlic, hot peppers, or
ginger are excellent here. Try the sizzling rice, when a scalding sauce
of shrimp and tomato is poured over deep-fried rice, or the smoked
duck, a Sichuan speciality flavoured with pungent wild Sichuan
peppercorns.

Suzhou

美味斋饭店　福州路 600 号
Meiweizhai Fandian 600 Fuzhou Road tel. 222258. Opened in
1926 this small restaurant is still going strong. It specializes in Suzhou
food, particularly in pork and other meat dishes. It also serves some
of the best Suzhou delicacies to be found in Shanghai: eel, shrimp,
and bean milk.

人民饭店　南京路
Renmin Fandian Nanjing Road tel. 537351. Although neither the
food nor the atmosphere can rival the best restaurants in Suzhou,
this restaurant near the Renmin Park offers a chance to try some of
the famous Suzhou dishes, such as 'squirrel' fish, sweet and sour

spareribs with a lemon-tinged sauce, and the delicately flavoured
'May' fish, a freshwater fish in season during the early part of
the summer.

Vegetarian

春风松月楼素荣馆 凝晖路 17 号
Chunfengsongyuelou Sucaiguan 17 Ninghui Road (inside the Old
Town market) tel. 289850. This is one of the three main vegetarian
restaurants in Shanghai (the Gongdelin and the Jade Buddha
Temple Suzhai are the other two.) It has been in business for
over 70 years. After a tour of the Old Town it is an excellent place
to stop for a meal. Any of its many beancurd dishes are highly
recommended.

功德林蔬食处 黄河路 43 号
Gongdelin Shushichu 43 Huanghe Road tel. 531313. This is the
best-known vegetarian restaurant in Shanghai. Vegetarian cooking is
a refined art in China and the Chinese are masters at producing an
astonishing variety of dishes from the versatile beancurd, the basis of
Chinese vegetarian cooking. A banquet in this attractive old
restaurant could consist of 15 courses of dishes that look as if they
are pork, duck, or fish, as well as plenty of deliciously fresh stir-fried
vegetables, many different kinds of mushrooms, seaweed, and, of
course, excellent noodles.

Western

锦江饭店 茂名路 59 号
Jinjiang Hotel 59 Maoming Road tel. 534242. Here also, both
Chinese and western cooking can always be relied upon to be good.
The European breakfasts are particularly to be recommended,
especially the excellent yoghurt which is not found in many
restaurants in China. The hotel's chefs have recently toured the
United States, demonstrating the best of China's cuisine. For
banquets, presentation and service in the palatial banqueting rooms
in the north building, where more than a thousand people can be
catered for, cannot be faulted.

国际饭店 南京西路 170 号
Park Hotel 170 Nanjing Road West tel. 563040. Foreign visitors
can now eat in what used to be called the Sky Terrace. On fine
summer nights a section of the ceiling would be rolled back and
patrons could dine and dance under the stars. Now it is simply a

restaurant, providing a wide choice of dishes, which are on the expensive side, although the portions are very generous.

和平饭店　南京东路 20 号

Peace Hotel 20 Nanjing Road East tel. 211244. The eighth-floor dining room in the north wing, because of its superb view down the Bund, is preferable to the first-floor dining room in the south wing, although the menus in both are the same. The menu is impressively comprehensive, offering several types of Chinese cuisine, as well as a large variety of western dishes.

Food in the general restaurants is always reliable, and served in the grand hotel style amongst ornate columns and chandeliers. The kitchen staff can also lay on a magnificent banquet in the elegant banqueting rooms on the hotel's upper floors.

红房子西餐馆　陕西南路 37 号

The Red House (Hong Fangzi) 37 Shaanxi Road South tel. 565748. Formerly known as Chez Louis, this intriguing anachronism has managed to survive the past 30 years as an entirely European restaurant — one of the few restaurants in Shanghai to do so. Hardly surprisingly, some of the dishes have become modified over the years, drifting away from their European models, but it is still fun to try onion soup, prawn salad, chicken piccata, or soufflé grand marnier, after a continuous diet of Chinese food. The restaurant,

Jinjiang Hotel

easily recognizable from its brightly painted red exterior, is only a few
minutes walk from the Jinjiang Hotel. Downstairs, groups of young
Chinese enthusiastically eat their way through their filet mignon and
crêpes suzettes, while upstairs, a quieter air-conditioned room is
reserved for foreign visitors. Prices are very high for China, and
service can be rather slow.

Coffee Shops and Snacks

Shanghai, described in the 1920s and '30s as the 'Paris of the East',
has not quite lost all that the name implies. In the city today there
are over 1800 coffee and pastry shops. They sell over 300 kinds of
snacks — everything from *Youtiao* (deep-fried twisted dough sticks),
dabing (a kind of large flatbread), or noodles in sauce to cakes,
dumplings and puddings. For an insight into how the people of
Shanghai live, it is well worth spending time in one of these coffee
shops. The clientele are generally friendly and eager to talk to
foreigners.

德大西菜社　四川中路359号
Deda Xicaishe 359 Sichuan Middle Road tel. 213810. The Deda
opened its doors to its first customers in 1897 and with very little
serious interruption the place has been doing good business ever
since. You can go to the second floor and have a fairly decent lunch
at a very reasonable price and then go downstairs for coffee and
cakes. It closes around 10pm and is always crowded. It is just a
minute's stroll from the Peace Hotel, on the corner of Sichuan
Middle Road and Nanjing Road East.

东海饭店　南京东路143号
Donghai Fandian 143 Nanjing Road East tel. 211940. Just down
the road from the Deda, the Donghai is a pastry and cake shop. The
restaurant opened in the 1930s and it, like the Deda, is still going
strong. Its speciality is cream cakes which, by any standards, are
very good. Though it is only a few doors away from the Deda the
customers are quite different — here family groups predominate.

凯歌　南京西路1001号
Kaige Coffee Shop 1001 Nanjing Road West tel. 535007. Originally
named the Kaiserling, the shop produces almost all of its own cakes
and pastries. Its cream cakes and fruit cakes are especially good.
The Kaige has another branch at Nanjing Road West just beside the
Xincheng swimming pool.

老大昌　淮海中路 377 号

Laodachang 377 Huaihai Middle Road tel. 374745. Come out of the main entrance of the Jinjiang Hotel and turn left, walk along Maoming Road until you reach Huaihai Middle Road and Laodachang is facing you on the opposite side of the street. Downstairs is the bakery and upstairs is the restaurant. A little grubbier than before 1949, neverthless for over 50 years it has been providing a fine service to those addicted to cream cakes, sweets, ice-cream and chocolate sundaes. The service is good and the prices are very reasonable. It is perhaps the best place of its kind in Shanghai.

上海咖啡馆　南京西路 1442 号 (铜仁路口)

Shanghai Coffee Shop 1442 Nanjing Road West (on the corner of Tongren Road) tel. 539893. This is a convenient coffee shop for those who have business at the Industrial Exhibition Hall. It is a clean place and one is made very welcome. It closes at 10.30 pm.

老城隍庙

Old Town Snacks In the oldest part of Shanghai, the Old Chinese City or Old Town as it is now known to foreigners, there are numerous snack shops. All of the snacks mentioned below can be found anywhere in Shanghai but the atmosphere in the Old Chinese City is unique. For early risers a trip to the Old City to have breakfast and watch the city come alive is one of the best experiences Shanghai offers — the best time to get there is between 6 and 7 am . You could start with dough balls filled with minced pork, or with noodle soup. Then you could move on to fried dumplings with beef and then glutinous rice in lotus leaves. You could of course forego all these and just munch on some sesame cakes and rolls. Recommended for breakfast any time are *youtiao* (deep-fried twisted dough sticks) which are delicious. There are many other equally enticing snacks awaiting those who wander through the streets and alleys of the Old Town. And the language barrier should not stop you; just point and you will be served with a smile.

Tightrope acrobat

Cultural Scene

Shanghai has been an important artistic centre for well over a century and, though there have been some major changes in political and social outlook, the city's cultural output is now richer than at any time since the Communist victory in 1949. All forms of art suffered during the Cultural Revolution (1966-76) but since the late 1970s theatres, cinemas, exhibition and concert halls have all taken on a new lease of life. Today local and foreign productions vie with each other for the headlines.

Foreign tourists in Shanghai tend to see only the shows that CITS select for them. But there are plenty of performances that the foreign visitor could go to on his own. Although a knowledge of Chinese is an obvious advantage, there is much that can be enjoyed without it. An evening at the theatre or cinema would give the traveller an opportunity to see another side of Shanghai life. It is also an excellent way of meeting people for there is always someone who wants to practise English.

Newspapers like *Wen Hui Bao* and the *Shanghai Evening News*, two of the local Chinese newspapers, always carry listings of what is on, but you will need help in reading them. The new English language newspaper *China Daily* also carries a few listings for Shanghai, and the paper can be bought in any major hotel. Tickets for shows can be bought through CITS or you can go directly to the theatre to buy them. Tickets for most shows go quickly, so if possible get them well in advance.

Shanghai has over 40 specialist companies and some ten important professional performing groups in everything from opera, ballet and music to comedy and acrobatics.

京剧

Jingju (Peking Opera) At the moment there are three Peking Opera troupes in Shanghai and all of them are working regularly in spite of a declining interest in traditional opera. Peking Opera is, however, the Chinese opera style probably best known to foreigners. It is highly formal and the stories come mostly from historical incidents or are based on specific characters with a tale written around them. Today there are also a number of operas based on modern heroes which are just as enjoyable as the old stories. The costumes are elaborate and extremely colourful.

昆剧

Kunju (Kunshan Opera) This opera form comes from around the Kunshan region in Jiangsu Province. It is a much less severe style than that of Peking and is more emotional and humorous. Although there is only one Kunju troupe in Shanghai at the moment it is one of the most popular opera forms.

沪剧

Huju (Shanghai Opera) Huju is Shanghai's most important local style of opera. It has developed its own particular characteristics over the years. In the past three decades Huju has taken a great deal from peasant arts and folklore, especially from the area of Jiangnan. In particular the songs, and the stage settings, are heavily influenced by the lifestyle to be found in Jiangnan. Huju is well-patronized in Shanghai and occasionally it can be difficult to get tickets so you should book ahead.

越剧

Yueju (Shaoxing Opera) Yueju form and style both date from the early 20th century and come from the town of Shaoxing in Jiangsu Province (the birthplace of China's most famous modern novelist, Lu Xun). Yueju is an opera form which is similar to standard theatre and, like the theatre, it was heavily influenced by the liberal May Fourth Movement of 1919. Yueju is an amusing style of opera and it is more relaxed than other forms. The sets are simple and the costumes colourful. Many of the stories are taken from modern and contemporary life in China.

淮剧

Huaiju (Northern Jiangsu Opera) Huaiju has a history going back some 200 years, but the Shanghai Huaiju Troupe was established only in 1951. Since the company came into existence it has per-formed widely and competed in most of the major opera competitions in China where it has gained a fine reputation.

滑稽戏

Huajixi (Farce) Farce is extremely popular in China and if you are travelling by train you will often hear it broadcast over the train's radio system. You are most likely to hear *Xiangsheng* which is a conversation between two men conducted at a very rapid pace. Farce uses many of the speech and movement techniques of classical theatre and opera as well as everyday body movements. Dialect and puns are a central part in the humour. Banned during the Cultural Revolution, farce has once again come into vogue and it is taken very seriously as an art form.

评弹

Pingtan This is a traditional art involving story-telling and ballad singing in the Suzhou dialect. Once seen everywhere in Shanghai, there is now a specialist touring troupe of around 18 people. The company, first established in 1951, is very popular. There are still a few people who perform in the streets of the city but this is rare. In the suburbs and in the countryside one may still see street performances. Pingtan is lively with much gesticulating and facial movement as befits the story being told. The ballads can be both sad and emotional at times.

木偶戏

Mu'ouxi (Puppets) One of the most famous of China's classical art forms, Mu'ouxi, like many other art forms, took a battering during the Cultural Revolution. Now it is slowly making a comeback in the ranks of popular culture. Today puppet shows are most often performed for children in their own theatres. But it is well worth going to a performance for Muouxi is one of the finest of arts. Adults may find it somewhat reminiscent of the Punch and Judy shows of their childhood.

电影

Cinema Once the film centre of China, Shanghai still has the reputation of producing not only the best films in the country but also the most experimental in both content and form. The Shanghai Film Studio at Xujiahui can be visited but you will have to apply through CITS. The major cinemas of Shanghai show a wide variety of Chinese films and, less frequently, foreign films. The foreign films shown on general release (and on television) are usually dubbed, although occasionally they may be subtitled. Tickets are very cheap and if the film is sold out there are always ticket touts operating outside the cinemas who will gladly provide you with one — at a price of course, but cheap all the same.

音乐

Music The Shanghai Orchestra is one of the best in the country. The orchestra had most of its instruments destroyed during the Cultural Revolution but in the last four years it has been revitalized and is now very busy. The guidance provided by the professors from the Shanghai Music College has formed the basis of their comeback, and standards have risen considerably. Visits from foreign orchestras, chamber music groups and individuals like Isaac Stern have also helped to improve the quality of performances. The Concert Hall on Yan'an Road holds regular concerts and it is best to book early, for the tickets go very quickly.

芭蕾舞

Ballet The Ballet Troupe of Shanghai acts also as the local dance school for Shanghai. Founded in 1966 the troupe has come a long way in perfecting its art but it is still far behind most well-known companies in the west, both in style and technique. The company has recently performed a number of ballets based on the works of the novelist, Lu Xun. Several dancers from the Shanghai Ballet Troupe have competed successfully in competitions abroad.

戏曲

Drama Huaju, or drama, has a relatively short history in China. The Shanghai Drama Troupe was founded in 1963. The Troupe up to now has specialized in historical plays but it has also performed a couple of controversial modern plays. Shakespeare has been produced successfully in Shanghai. Perhaps the most outstanding performance was that given by a group of Tibetan drama students who staged *Romeo and Juliet* in 1981. The People's Art Theatre Troupe, established in 1951, also produces plays, but again concentrates mostly on historical drama. Recently, though, a play from Taiwan was performed at the Arts Theatre on Maoming Road.

杂技

Acrobatics The Shanghai Acrobatic Troupe is world famous and almost everyone who visits Shanghai will go to see them. It is a performance which leaves one stunned by the sheer versatility and power of the troupe and will make any visit to Shanghai memorable.

争分夺秒 奔向2000！

Demonstration of swordsmanship

Church and Worship

Before 1949 there were more than 300 congregations in Shanghai
which included Protestant, Roman Catholic, Islamic, Russian
Orthodox, Jewish, Buddhist and Japanese Shinto. Today, however,
for Shanghai's Christian population there are only eight Protestant
churches and one Catholic church open for services. An indefinite
number of other churches are due to be renovated and reopened for
worship during 1983.

Anyone interested in seeing what Shanghai is like on Sunday
mornings for many Shanghainese would find a visit to a church
worthwhile. It can be a moving experience to witness the faithful
participating in an aspect of their lives which has been so long
denied them. It is best to go as early as possible in the morning,
around 7.30 am, to get a good seat. Foreigners will always be made
extremely welcome.

Shanghai's large Moslem community — which is made up
mostly of people from China's northwestern province of Xinjiang —
is currently served by only one mosque. There are no longer any
synagogues in Shanghai and the city's Jewish community, which
was quite large before 1949, no longer exists. There is, however, a
beautiful Russian Orthodox church which is worth visiting even
though it is now used as a warehouse. It is on Xinle Road, a couple
of blocks from the Jinjiang Club. Go down Changle Road, and turn
left by the Red House Restaurant. Then walk two blocks to Xinle
Road and turn right. The church is about half way down the street.

International Church (also known today as Community Church)
53 Hengshan Road. This is the Protestant church perhaps best
known to foreigners. A No. 42 bus will take you there from the
Bund and it stops right by the church.

Services: Sunday 7.30 am and 10.00 am.

Kunshan Protestant Church Kunshan Road. This delightful
church was reopened in late 1981 and is located on the north side
of Suzhou Creek. To reach it take a No. 55 bus which goes to
Wujiaochang. Take the bus a half-a-dozen stops up to Wusong
Road and get off just past Kunshan Road. Then walk back about 20
yards and turn right onto Kunshan Road. The small church is about
half way up the street and it cannot be missed.

Services: Sunday 7.30 am and 9.30 am. There is also a regular
evening service. This church has four pastors looking after it.

Mosque Fuyou Road. This mosque currently serves Shanghai's Moslem community. It is a modern building and is only recognizable as a mosque by the green tablet over the door. Services are at the standard times of the day for Moslems.

Xujiahui Catherdral (St. Ignatius Cathedral) The cathedral is one of Shanghai's most famous landmarks. Reopened in November 1979, it has space for 2500 people but at any important festival there are always a good many more. Built in 1906, the cathedral has had an interesting history, particularly during the Cultural Revolution (1966-1976) when it was closed and parts of it were destroyed by the Red Guards. To give one some idea of the hold of the Catholic Church in present-day Shanghai one ought to go to a service here. At Christmas as many as 12,000 people come to worship and it is almost impossible to get through the crowds who gather in and around the church. In the church grounds there are make-shift stalls which sell a wide range of religious paraphernalia. Located in the southwest of the city it can be reached by taking a No. 26 bus. Get off at the last bus stop at Xujiahui and it is about 200 yards down the road on the right.

Services: There are five services every Sunday morning beginning at 4.45 am. The last one is at 9.30 am.

Zhabei Church 8 Baotong Road. This Protestant church is a 15-minute walk north from the main railway station. It was reopened on 25 July, 1982 after being closed for 16 years. The outside is painted a creamy colour which throws the church into stark contrast with the run-down air of the surrounding area. Above the entrance are large red Chinese characters denoting the name of the church and above the characters hangs a large red cross. Inside there are rows of simple wooden pews with space for some 700 worshippers. During the services there is a small choir of nine women and eight men who perform to the accompaniment of a single piano.

Services: Sunday 7.30 am and 9.30 am. There is also the occasional evening service. Communion is by invitation only, though foreigners are always made welcome by the two pastors who look after the church.

Fabric store

Shopping

An Introduction to Shopping in Shanghai

By Lynn M. Osen

Shanghai is not only China's greatest commercial centre, but also one of the country's major sources of production. And, with more than 24,000 shops, it is small wonder that the city enjoys a reputation as China's best shopping centre. The Chinese expect to find here a wider range of better quality goods to buy than in any other city in China. The fashions are considered to be the most modern in China and the design and quality of many of the consumer goods produced here are thought to be superior.

For the foreign visitor, the overwhelmingly commercial atmosphere of the city usually proves infectious. Whatever you are interested in buying in China — anything from antiques to inexpensive souvenirs — it is well worthwhile seeing what Shanghai's shops have to offer.

The city's busiest and most exciting shopping area is at the east end of Nanjing Road. Over 400 stores line this famous street which sells just about every consumer item that China produces. It runs west for over six miles from the waterfront, dividing the city in two. The second major shopping area is in the heart of the old French Concession around Huaihai Road, southwest of Nanjing Road East. Here it is possible to shop, in slightly less crowded conditions, in a vast variety of stores, including the well-known department store catering only for women.

Some of the hotels where foreign visitors stay are within comfortable walking distance of the larger department stores of Nanjing Road, or of the Friendship Store in Zhongshan Number One Road East. But, whichever hotel you stay in, it is always easy and inexpensive to take a taxi. The hotel reception desk will call a taxi and explain to the driver where you want to go. The reception desk or your Chinese guide will also write out instructions in Chinese for the driver to be used later in the journey.

Many foreign visitors will find that shopping in Shanghai or elsewhere in China is not simply a self-indulgent pastime for the opulent tourist. For many it represents one of the best opportunities to gain an insight into the Chinese lifestyle, the cost of living and the state of the country's technological development.

Shopping in Friendship Stores For those not familiar with Friendship Stores, these are officially established outlets for items sold directly to foreign visitors. There is a Friendship Store in each of the Chinese cities open to tourists, offering a wide variety of products not always available in the local shops.

There are several advantages to shopping in Friendship Stores. The sales staff, for instance, have some facility (albeit scant at times) in other languages. The merchandise offered is generally of better quality than that found in local stores, and there is also a greater variety of merchandise designed for western use. Most of the larger Friendship Stores will also assist in packing and shipping items home, though this may be time-consuming to arrange.

Prices are fixed — as they are in local department stores — so bargaining is of course unnecessary. But the prices in the Friendship Stores do tend to be higher than in the local shops, and, if you are leaving or entering China through Hong Kong, it also is worthwhile making a comparison with prices in the very reasonable China Products stores there.

It was announced in April 1980 that goods in Friendship Stores were to be paid for with foreign currency certificates. There are facilities for exchanging travellers cheques in Friendship Stores — a process not always possible in department stores. A few Stores, including the one in Shanghai, now issue foreign currency certificates to credit card holders, but you should check with your credit card company or bank before you rely on this form of payment for your purchases.

It is worth remembering that since many of the items are produced regionally — or even individually in the case of artwork — it is always advisable to buy as soon as you find what you want. The same items do not always appear again in Friendship Stores in other cities.

Shanghai's Friendship Store The Friendship Store is at 33 Zhongshan Number One Road East, between the Peace Hotel and Shanghai Mansions, set back from the road in the grounds of the former British Consulate. To reach the store, follow the drive round to the left after walking through the large entrance gates.

The first floor of the Friendship Store displays small goods such as handbags, clocks, calculators, watches and toys. The labels alone of many of these Chinese products are worth looking at — even the most mundane articles have exotic brand names such as Winged Tiger, Double Horse, White Mountain, Pansy, Panda, or Snowflake.

The upper floors of the store offer a more luxurious choice of items. Here you can find thick, hand-cut rugs, heavily lacquered and carved teak furniture, coromandel screens embossed with jade or ivory figures, and ivory or wood carvings. There is also an almost endless selection of jewelry incorporating precious and semi-precious stones — jade, rose quartz, lapis lazuli, pearls, and diamonds, set in gold or silver. Jewelry prices are fairly reasonable, compared with those in the west, and most of the stones are quite good.

In the clothing department, men's wear includes silk, cotton and polyester shirts as well as cashmere sweaters, scarves, gloves and underwear. For women, there are blouses in heavily embroidered silk, linen and cotton, cashmere items, silk gowns and soft velvet slippers embroidered in silk.

It is possible to have a 'Mao suit' made to order here. But for any custom-made clothing, it is worthwhile remembering that the tailor uses Japanese patterns which need modification to suit the taller and longer-waisted frame of the westerner.

For those who live in colder climates, there are fur coats and jackets, both ready-to-wear and custom-made. Many of these have steep five-figure price tags, but the selection is ample.

Both Shanghai and Hangzhou manufacture some of the best silk to be found in China. Bolts of silk are on sale in the Friendship Store in every conceivable weave from soft crêpe de Chine to heavy brocade. There are also exquisitely hand-embroidered linens, sheets, table-cloths and bedcovers, all available in a variety of materials with artwork, trapunto or appliqué designs, and costing only a fraction of the price of similar luxury items in the west.

Antiques Inveterate antique-hunters may at first be disappointed by the small number of antique shops in China. But it has to be remembered that for almost 30 years the Chinese government, realising the enormous export potential of selling Chinese antiquities, has been systematically collecting antiques, and offering them to foreign dealers in wholesale lots. Nowadays, however, with the rapid expansion of the tourist industry, more antiques and secondhand goods are being diverted from these wholesale lots and are finding their way into retail antique shops, set up specially for the foreign visitors.

There are three main antique shops in Shanghai where foreign visitors are likely to be taken — the Antiques and Curios Branch of the Friendship Store at 694 Nanjing Road West, the antique section of the Friendship Store in Zhongshan Number One Road East and the Shanghai Antiques and Curios Store at 218-226 Guangdong Road, not far from Nanjing Road East. Many feel that the antiques offered for sale in Shanghai are amongst the best in range and quality to be found in China's retail stores.

In general, the bulk of the antiques that the non-specialist foreign visitor will come across will date from the late Qing period (the second half of the 19th century) through to the days of the Japanese occupation. When buying antiques it is probably wiser to concentrate more on the quality of the piece rather than on its age.

Any article purchased as an antique for export should bear a red wax seal. Special customs declaration forms are available in the antique shops, although the wax seal is usually enough to convince most customs officers that the article is not liable for duty in those countries exempting antiques. All sales receipts should be kept to show on departure from China.

Shanghai's antique stores offer good selections of old porcelain and cloisonné pieces — vases, plates, bowls and so on. It is also worth looking at their attractive collections of old scrolls, paintings and prints. There are numerous old pieces of carved jade and ivory figures, perfume bottles and intricately carved seals in everything from wood to the finest jade which are accompanied by the small porcelain ink pots in wooden boxes for use with the seals.

The antique stores also carry interesting selections of old silk embroideries. There are small panels suitable for framing as well as larger pieces. The gloriously-coloured skirts are particularly attractive. Many of them are large enough to make impressive wallhangings but for the extravagant or indulgent, there are some that might be worn as elegant ballgowns.

The stores have a variety of antique jewelry, peking glass, and small, carved jade pieces ideal to wear on gold chains or as bracelet charms. There is a wealth of other exotica to look at, such as the wide rings once used by royal archers to protect their fingers, or small engraved boxes which held the scented wax the archers used on their crossbows.

A few excellent reproductions can be found in Shanghai's antique shops. There are, for instance, superb pottery figures of Tang horses better than those available in Xi'an or in Peking's famous antique street Liulichang. Some of the ceramic figures have taken a year or more to complete and the artisans have accurately reproduced the soft, dusty shadings that give the pieces a convincing look of age.

Shopping in department stores Shanghai has long been famous for its vast department stores. In the '30s and '40s you could supposedly find anything you wanted in the celebrated Wing On Department Store in Nanjing Road — now simply called Number 10 Department Store — which sold everything from ivory back-scratchers and mink coats to green envelopes and violet ice-cream. Today, in striking contrast to the exotic and cosmopolitan range of merchandise available in Shanghai before 1949, the stores sell, with a few exceptions, only Chinese-produced goods. But the city's numerous department stores are just as large, and their turnover is enormous. Shanghai's biggest store — the Number One Department Store in Nanjing Road East — claims to offer over 36,000 different commodities, and serves 100,000 customers a day — with double that number actually visiting the store. A visit to this, or any other of the large department stores, is the ideal opportunity to look at the range of consumer products available in China, and check the prices of the domestic market.

When buying in department stores (or in the smaller local shops), it is worth saving the sales slips, and, most importantly, identifying each item on the slip at the time of purchase. Invoices are usually written in Chinese characters, and customs officers back home may not take kindly to holding up a long line while purchases are matched with indecipherable sales slips.

It is also important not to be upset if the local shoppers stand aside so that the foreigners may be served first. This is the custom and you should accept graciously, otherwise the floor manager will insist. The practice has less to do with deference than with expediency, the assumption being that foreigners have less time for shopping than local citizens have.

Number One Department Store The store is on four floors, with very crowded stairways between each floor. There are also elevators reserved for foreign shoppers.

Pottery and porcelain shop

As you enter the front door, on the right is the linen counter with a slightly different selection of hand-embroidered work than the embroidery available at the Friendship Store. Household items can be great bargains here. Prices are very low and the fabrics range from cotton, silk and linen to a variety of man-made fibres. Polyester or synthetic fabrics should be embroidered with polyester thread. If cotton thread has been used with synthetic fibre, it may shrink in the heat of modern dryers giving the embroidery an uneven look. Some stores may require ration coupons for cotton articles. Your Chinese guide can usually provide these, although, in the past, most of Shanghai's stores have not required them.

On the first floor you will find luxurious goose-down quilts with silk, rayon or cotton covers. These sell for considerably less than western prices and the sales staff here seem to be very skilful at binding them into surprisingly compact rolls for easy packing.

In the first-floor children's department the tiny jeans and blouses are beautifully embroidered. The small padded jackets that keep the children warm in the bitterly cold winter months are also worth looking at.

T-shirts with pictures of Shanghai stencilled across the front are on sale on this floor, and so are the popular Shanghai bags. These are made of heavy khaki canvas with a rubberized backing and have the name and picture of the city stencilled on the side. They are available for a few *yuan* each. If you need an extra bag, then these are ideal — particularly if you also buy one of the tiny brass locks on sale at the luggage counter in the basement.

At the tea department on the first floor you can buy the prized chrysanthemum tea harvested in nearby Hangzhou. Available in bulk or in colourful canisters, it is one of the many types of tea sold in the store. The practical covered cups used by the Chinese to keep their tea warm are on sale in the basement, together with the large enamel, or straw-covered thermos flasks used everywhere in China. Sewing machines, bicycles, luggage, and hardware are also displayed in the basement.

The clothing department on the second floor offers the hand-embroidery so popular on all fabric garments. Here, there are women's blouses and slips, along with acres of cotton, silk, and brocade material — some of it surprisingly sumptuous. Weightless padded jackets are available in silk, satin, or brocade, most of them filled with the finest goose down or with silk wadding. If you are interested in cashmere sweaters, then check out this department on the second floor, where prices are better than in the Friendship Store and the selection is more extensive. Even heavy-knit sweaters for men are relatively inexpensive but also look for scarves, gloves, socks, and underwear in this luxury fabric. Camel-hair sweaters are also available during the cold months.

At the shoe counters on the second floor, the sales lady will bring you a wooden stool to sit on while you try on the blunt-toed, single-strap shoes so popular with Chinese men and women. They come in a variety of fabrics ranging from leather to corduroy and velvet.

The top floor has a counter where signature seals may be made to order with your own name or initials carved into the stone. They are available in jade, ivory, marble, agate, serpentine or soapstone. Patterns are endless — some may be topped with the popular Chinese lion emblem, while others have a Chinese scene etched into the side of the seal. These make excellent gifts and can be very inexpensive. They are also easy to pack. But since they are specially cut to order, allow at least 24 to 48 hours for this process. If the department store cannot meet a particular deadline, try at a smaller street shop where business may not be as heavy and schedules are more flexible. The store does have a few antique seals — most of them jade or other precious stones — but these are quite expensive.

Musicians will be entranced by the array of strange musical instruments on the top floor. The most popular of these is the *erhu*, a two-stringed instrument played like a violin. Chinese records are also for sale in this department and a recording of 'The East is Red' is sure to evoke memories in years to come.

In addition, the top floor has an extensive display of statues, carvings, paintings, scrolls and other fine art pieces produced by modern artists.

Painting and calligraphy shops You need not be an artist to enjoy the products in these stores. Reams of beautiful handmade paper, envelopes, folders and cards can be bought for next to nothing. They also sell intriguing writing instruments and artists' supplies. Particularly appealing are the small clay intaglio forms used for printing, which, when backed and framed properly, make very attractive wall hangings. There are brushes of all kinds and sizes made of everything from hand-drawn boar's bristles and goat hair to the finest pure sable or young camel hair. Western stores sell these brushes at scandalous prices for use as cosmetics brushes.

Speciality shops Some of the most interesting bargains to be had in Shanghai are in the many smaller speciality shops in and around Nanjing Road East. Here you can find silk socks for men, or sandalwood fans, acupuncture dolls, opera costumes, or an embroidered silk down-filled baby carrier.

For cutlery, knives and scissors, try number 490 Nanjing Road East, or, if you are interested in the martial arts, look at the shop

Painting and calligraphy shop, Nanjing Road

specializing in *wushu* equipment at 259 Nanjing Road East. Number 118 has an excellent selection of Chinese and western musical instruments, while number 309 specializes in Chinese flags and banners. Number 422, Duoyunxuan, is an attractive old shop specializing in prints and scrolls by famous artists. With its fine wooden panelling, and wooden gallery around the second floor, the shop itself is worth looking at, even if you are not interested in buying. And, whatever your age, toy shops are sure to be rewarding stops. Look for the enormous variety of small metal toys, or the stuffed pandas, and irresistible comic ducks and bears in shops such as the one near the Peace Hotel, at 98 Nanjing Road.

Those who sew might find a swatch of batik, silk ribbons, or spools of colourful silk thread in one of the many specialist sewing shops. The Chinese are said to have invented thimbles and these can be found in highly decorated designs, together with bone, ivory, or jade buttons.

Bookshops One obligatory stop is the bookstore. Try the excellent Xinhua Bookstore at 345 Nanjing Road East, or the Foreign Languages Bookstore in Fuzhou Road. There is also a convenient bookshop for those staying at the Jinjiang Hotel, right in the hotel's compound. These bookshops all have a wide range of publications from Peking's prolific Foreign Languages Press, which produces books in several languages and has a very large selection in English. Some are massive works of art, while others are small paperbacks covering a range of specialized interests from agriculture and archaeology to the status of women in China.

Look here also for papercuts, those intricate hand-cut designs the Chinese use for decorating everything from thermoses to shop windows. Bookshops also stock dictionaries, attractive calendars, stamp collections, picture postcards from every large city in China, and posters. Be sure to pick up a map of China, or one of the world seen through Chinese eyes.

Chinese medicines and cosmetics The small shops selling herbs and medicines are fascinating. Here you can buy ivory dust, ground horn, and other exotic curatives such as 'Lady Bloom' or ginseng extracts. For those interested in cooking, saffron, considered to be a medicinal herb by the Chinese, can be bought here at bargain prices. The Number One Chemist Store, near the Number One Department Store, has the best stock of both western and Chinese medicines.

Cosmetics are becoming increasingly more available, and, quite naturally in the city that leads China's fashion, lipsticks and face powder are appearing in many shops. But foreign visitors used to their own brands would of course be well-advised to bring a supply of all their medical and cosmetic needs with them.

Jade Tour groups to Shanghai are sometimes taken to visit one of the city's jade factories, where workers shape and polish jade into consumer items. Some of these creations take months, even years, to perfect and are considerable works of art. Small shops attached to the factories display a collection of their products at understandably steep prices.

If you are planning to buy any jade in China, it would be advisable to learn ahead of time as much as possible about it. Learn how to tell the difference between jadeite and nephrite, what the Chinese call true jade or *zhen yu,* and what minerals give shadings to the stone. X-ray diffraction is the only infallible way to judge jade with precision, so unless you simply fall in love with a certain piece and do not mind the price, such investments should be made very carefully.

Lynn M. Osen is an author and lecturer at the University of California, Irvine Campus. After spending four years in the Far East, she has developed a keen interest in the orient, and now visits China regularly.

Shanghai's Main Shopping Streets

Nanjing Road

One of the best ways of getting to know any city is by taking to its streets. Shanghai boasts a number of attractive streets which are ideal for the imaginative shopper and for general exploring. Nanjing Road is divided into two sections: Nanjing Road East and Nanjing Road West, formerly known as Bubbling Well Road which began at the International (Park) Hotel. Stretching for six miles, from the Bund to Jiangsu Road, Nanjing Road was, and still is, Shanghai's largest shopping street. With almost 400 shops it is a consumer's paradise, offering an enormous range of standard goods as well as many more unusual items.

Before 1949, Nanjing Road was the street of the famous Wing On Department Store, restaurants of all kinds — Chinese, Russian, French, American — and of smart hotels and popular nightclubs. Today it is still Shanghai's busiest street, constantly jammed with pedestrians and crowded buses; bicycles have been banned from the street until the quieter evening hours. Nanjing Road still contains numerous restaurants, cinemas, coffee shops, and the circular theatre where the Shanghai Acrobatic Company performs its feats of skill and daring. The skyline of the road is now dominated by the nearby Television Tower, 750 feet high, built in 1975, and daily relaying programmes in colour.

Nanjing Road is the street of the famous **Number One and Number Ten Department Stores** and the **Duoyunxuan Painting and Calligraphy Store,** but there are many other shops which are worth looking into for the range of goods and services they provide.

As an alternative to the Duoyunxuan Paintings and Calligraphy Store, the **Shanghai Arts and Crafts Store** at 190-208 Nanjing Road West (tel. 531796) offers a broad range of interesting papercuts, scrolls and wall mountings. For porcelain and pottery there are three stores that one might try: **Guohua Porcelain Shop** which is located at 550 Nanjing Road East (tel. 224526), **Shanghai Jingdezhen Porcelain Artware Service** at 1175 Nanjing Road West (tel. 530885) and **Huashan Pottery and Porcelain Shop** at 1698 Nanjing Road West (tel. 539350).

The **Xinhua Bookstore** at 345 Nanjing Road East is the main branch office for all Xinhua bookstores in Shanghai. The shop is on two floors and though they are spacious and well-arranged they are usually very crowded. On the first floor you will find the periodicals section to the right as you enter; on the left there is the children's book section and beside this the music section with a variety of western and Chinese music on cassette. On the second floor is the main section of the bookstore where you can buy novels, books on science and politics, dictionaries, maps, posters and Chinese books in Braille. Tucked away in the far corner of the second floor is a section for foreigners where you will find a variety of books, paper-cuts, paintings and postcards. For children's books try the **Children's Bookstore** located at 722 Nanjing Road West (tel. 533467).

Also for children there is the **Shanghai Children's Shoes and Hats Shop** at 600 Nanjing Road East (tel. 229850) where there is a good general selection of children's wear. At the **Xingyang Children's Shop** located at 993 Nanjing Road West (tel. 562422) there is a wide range of clothing, toys and children's furniture which would make delightful presents.

An alternative general department store can be found at the **Shanghai Overseas Chinese Store** at 627 Nanjing Road East (tel. 225424). It is just next to the Number Ten Department Store.

Shanghai is known throughout China as the most fashionable city in the country and has an enormous number of specialist clothing stores. The **Shanghai Fabric Store** at 592 Nanjing Road East is considered one of the best places for silks. These come in varied colours and weights and the staff will help you to make your selection. There is also a range of cotton goods which are fairly inexpensive. The **New Woman's Clothing Store** at 750 Nanjing Road East (tel. 22193) offers good service and a wide selection of ready-to-wear styles. For jewelry the **Shanghai Jewelry Store** at 428 Nanjing Road East (tel. 224776) will provide you with a good selection.

For camera and photographic supplies and repairs try the **Guanlong Photographic Supplies Shop** at 180 Nanjing Road East (tel. 210882/214015). First opened in 1931, the shop will repair almost any kind of camera quickly and efficiently. They also sell a variety of accessories and developing materials including Seagull paper for black and white prints which is reputed to be outstanding in quality and difficult to find. Further down the road there is the **Scene Photo Materials Shop** at 258 Nanjing Road West (tel. 538374) which offers materials and services similar to those at the Guanlong.

There are many shops specializing in both western and Chinese musical instruments but among the best is the **Shanghai National Music Store** at 114 Nanjing Road East (tel. 213869). Staff at this shop are particularly knowledgeable and the service is good.

The **Shanghai Sporting Goods Store** at 160 Nanjing Road East (tel. 214789) is one of the best of its kind in Shanghai. If they do not have what you are after they will give you directions to other stores which might be able to help. If you buy a tracksuit at this shop

Trolleybus, Nanjing Road

and want your name or university printed on it in Chinese characters they will do it for a small charge.

On a hot sticky day in Shanghai — and there are many of those — a hairwash and head massage is an ideal way to cool down and relax. In addition to the barbers and women's hairdressers in the large hotels there are some 700 barber and hairdresser shops in Shanghai, everything from the simple street-corner barber to the comfortable old-world charm of the Nanjing Road barber shops. The **Nanjing Barber Shop** at 786 Nanjing Road West (tel. 532958) is one of the city's most popular, catering to a wide clientele and trying hard to meet their more ambitious demands. But the most famous barber in Shanghai is undoubtedly the **Xin Xin Barber Shop** at 546 Nanjing Road East (tel. 223284). The Xin Xin employs 71 hairdressers who have all been trained in Shanghai and have specialized in male or female styles during their three years of study. The men's barber is on the first floor and the ladies' shop is on the second floor. On the third floor there is a perm room and beauty parlour. At US$1.00, a shave and head and chest massage is a good bargain by any standards. Women can spend up to US$5.00 for a complete hairdo with a manicure and make-up. An alternative for men is the **Hua'an Barber Shop** at 104 Nanjing Road West (tel. 226718).

Huaihai Road
Huaihai Road is almost as long as Nanjing Road. The centrepiece of the former French Concession, Huaihai Road has had five names, including its present one, during its lifetime: the two most famous were Avenue Joffre and Xiafei Road. The road is divided into three sections — East, Middle and West — but it is only the East and Middle Roads which are of real interest to the shopper. The shopping area stretches from Xizang Road where Huaihai Road East begins, some seven blocks west from the Peace Hotel, and stops at Xiangyang Road South where Huaihai Middle Road ends. In this stretch of road there are some 200 shops of which more than 50 are specialist clothing or footwear shops.

Convenient for those who are at the Jinjiang Hotel, the street offers some of the best shopping in town and is just a little less crowded than Nanjing Road. For those interested in ceramics and porcelain the **Chuanxin Shop,** at 1297 Huaihai Road, offers a good selection. This shop also has a stock of pewter and lacquerware which is worth looking at. The **Yuhua Arts and Crafts Store** at 933 Huaihai Middle Road is also a good shop for bargain-hunters.

At 722 Huaihai Middle Road (tel. 211854) the **Shanghai Changjiang Seal Carving Factory** is worth visiting. Seal carving has a long and honoured history in China. In the old days seals were used for everything from marking a painting to sealing bills, cheques and contracts (this is still done in Taiwan). At this seal carving factory you may select from a wide range of high quality wood or stone seals and, if you give your name in Chinese characters, have it carved on the seal of your choice.

Numerous small side streets in the Huaihai Road area have secondhand stores selling some interesting furniture and antiques. For old furniture try the small alley tucked away out of sight behind the Commission Shop at 426 Huaihai Middle Road.

Fuzhou Road and Yan'an Road

Fuzhou Road runs parallel to Nanjing Road. Running down from the Bund to the People's Square, Fuzhou Road is known primarily for its bookshops, papershops and artworks stores. Its bookshops are particularly popular and occasionaly there are rarities among the old books, especially the foreign books which were taken from private libraries during the Cultural Revolution (1966-1976).

At the **China Classics Bookstore** at 424 Fuzhou Road (tel. 223453/224984), you will find an excellent selection of books in classical Chinese as well as calligraphy and paintings, rubbings and seals. The **Shanghai Bookstore** at 401-411 Fuzhou Road (tel. 282894), originally called the Shanghai Old Bookstore, has a large collection of old books and periodicals with many outlets throughout the city. It is a good place to hunt around for out-of-print books. The store itself has recently been renovated and is now much pleasanter than before. It is best to go early on in the day since the store gets busy very quickly. The **Foreign Languages Bookstore** at 390 Fuzhou Road (tel. 224109) has also undergone recent renovation and is now a spacious bookshop with a wide range of periodicals and books in French, German, English and Spanish.

For those with an interest in Chinese painting the **Shanghai Art Supplies Store** is a fairly small but well-stocked store. The brushes range from middling quality to excellent; ink and inkstones are also available. The service is very good and one is always made welcome.

Yan'an Road was formerly a creek but was filled in during the 19th century and came to form the boundary between the French Concession and the International Settlement. Today it is one of the major thoroughfares in Shanghai.

One of the shops of most interest to tourists is the **Shaanxi Old Wares Store** at 557 Yan'an Middle Road (tel. 565489). It is well stocked with antique furniture, curios, jewelry and nicknacks.

Bicycle park attendants

NANJING ROAD EAST AND THE BUND
南京东路 – 外滩

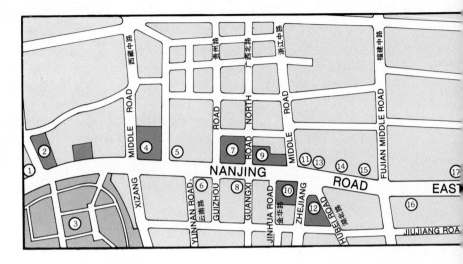

1. Shanghai Arts and Crafts Store
   上海工艺美术品服务部
2. Park Hotel 国际饭店
3. Renmin Park 人民公园
4. Number One Department Store
   第一百货店
5. Wangxingji Fan Shop 王星记扇庄
6. Yanyunlou Mandarin Restaurant 燕云楼
7. Number One Food Store 第一食品商店
8. Xinya Cantonese Restaurant 新雅粤菜馆
9. Shanghai Clothing Store 上海服装商店
10. Number Ten Department Store
    第十百货店
11. Shanghai Number One Chemist Store
    上海市第一医药商店
12. Shanghai Overseas Chinese Store
    上海华侨商店
13. Shanghai Silk Shop 上海绸缎商店
14. Guohua Porcelain Shop 国华瓷器商店
15. Xin Xin Barber Shop 新新美发厅
16. Sichuan Restaurant 四川饭店
17. Duoyunxuan Painting and Calligraphy
    Store 朵云轩

18. Xinhua Bookstore 新华书店
19. Youyi Photography Shop 友谊照相馆
20. Yangzhou Restaurant 扬州饭店
21. Shanghai Theatre Shop
    上海戏剧刀枪门市部
22. Laojiefu Silk Shop 老介福呢绒绸缎商店
23. Philately Shop 中国邮票公司上海市分公
24. Guanlong Photographic Supplies Shop
    冠龙照相器材商店
25. Shanghai Sporting Goods Store
    上海体育用品商店
26. Typewriter Store 上海打字机商店
27. Donghai Coffee Shop 东海饭店
28. Shanghai National Music Store
    上海民族乐器一厂服务部
29. Haida Shirt Shop 海达衬衫商店
30. Deda Restaurant 德大西菜社
31. Chen Lie Crafts 市手工业局产品陈列室
32. Peace Hotel 和平饭店
33. Friendship Store 友谊商店
34. Huangpu Park 黄浦公园

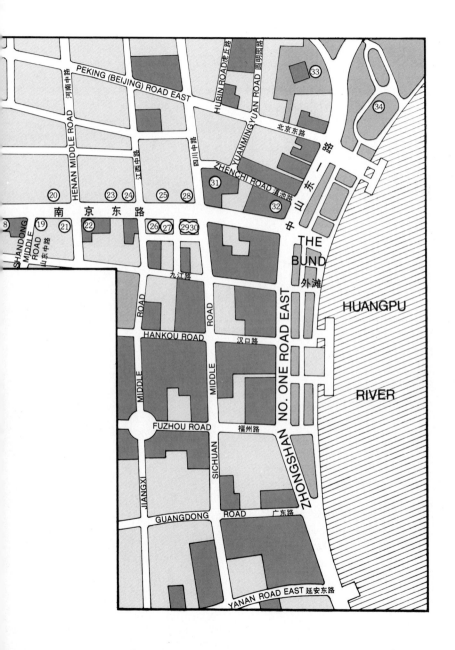

NANJING ROAD WEST 南京西路

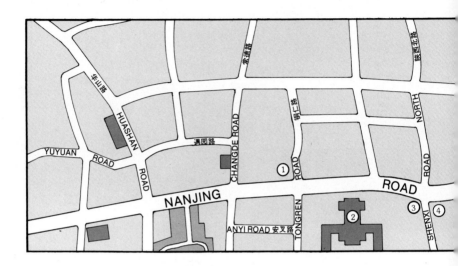

1. Shanghai Coffee Shop 上海咖啡馆
2. Shanghai Industrial Exhibition Hall 上海工业展览馆
3. Pingan Cinema 平安影院
4. Shanghai Jingdezhen Porcelain Artware Service 上海景德镇艺术瓷器服务部
5. Meilongzhen Restaurant 梅龙镇酒家
6. Kaige Coffee Shop 凯歌
7. Shanghai Children's Food Shop 上海儿童食品商店
8. Xiangyang Children's Shop 向阳儿童用品商店
9. Nanjing Barber Shop 南京理发店
10. Children's Bookstore 少年儿童书店
11. Luyangcun Restaurant 绿杨村饭店
12. Xinhua Cinema 新华影院

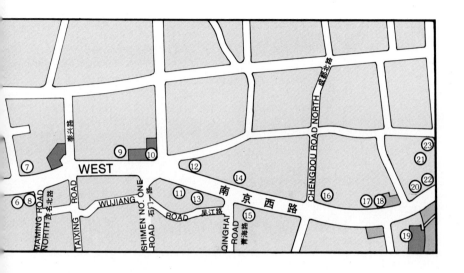

13. Shanghai Photographic Shop　上海照相馆
14. Friendship Antiques and Curios Store　友谊古玩分店
15. TV Tower　电视台
16. Shanghai Art Exhibition Hall　上海美术展览馆
17. Acrobatics Theatre　杂技场
18. Flower and Bird Shop　上海花鸟商店
19. Shanghai Library　上海图书馆
20. Renmin Fandian　人民饭店
21. Changjiang Theatre　长江剧场
22. Daguangming Cinema　大光明影院
23. Gongdelin Vegetarian Restaurant　功德林素食处

HUAIHAI MIDDLE ROAD 淮海中路

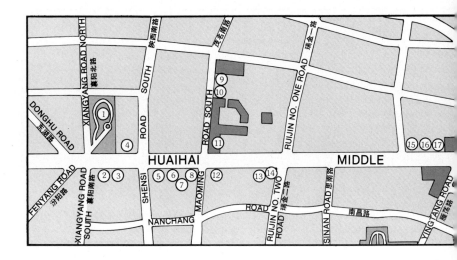

1. Xiangyan Park 襄阳公园
2. Tianjinguan Restaurant   天津馆
3. Shanghai Food Shop 上海食品厂
4. Huaihai Photographic Shop 淮海照相馆
5. Yuhua Arts and Crafts Shop 玉华工艺品商店
6. Ha'erbin Food Shop   哈尔滨食品厂
7. Number Two Department Store 上海市第二百货商店
8. Laodachang Coffee Shop 老大昌
9. Jinjiang Hotel   锦江饭店
10. Jinjiang Club 锦江俱东部

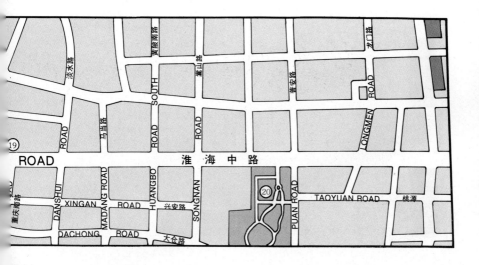

11. Guotai Cinema 国泰影院
12. Shanghai Western Food Restaurant   上海西菜社
13. Chengdu Restaurant 成都饭店
14. Haiyan Food Shop 海燕食品厂
15. Huaihai Cinema 淮海影院
16. Hongyi Photographic Supply Shop 红艺照相材料商店
17. Qilin Department Store 麒麟百货商店
18. Shanghai Women's Store 上海市妇女用品商店
19. Huaihai Secondhand Shop   淮海旧货商店
20. Huaihai Park 淮海公园

Longhua Pagoda

Sights in Shanghai

Children's Palaces

In a scheme to allow children a chance to develop interests outside their school work — whether it be painting, music, physics, gymnastics, model-aeroplanes, table-tennis or ballet — Shanghai has developed its system of children's palaces. Each of Shanghai's 10 urban districts organizes a palace where children go for several hours a week after school, and there is one run by the Municipality. The palaces are staffed by volunteer teachers from the schools, as well as some full-time instructors.

A visit to one of the palaces is a particularly enjoyable part of any tour itinerary in Shanghai. Visitors usually watch some of the children's classes, and are then given a display of some sort by the children. The palaces differ enormously in quality of facilities, and in the type of child that attends. The most spectacular is the Municipal Palace, which occupies the house where the influential and wealthy Kadoorie family of Hong Kong used to live. The children who attend have been handpicked for their outstanding abilities, and it is here that you will come across those widely-publicized little child prodigies.

Factories

Shanghai's industrial production is greater than that of any other municipality, province or autonomous region in China. And this is despite a government policy over the past 30 years of deliberately trying to build up other industrial bases in China, and limiting the growth of China's biggest city.

Since 1949, industrial progress in the city has been spectacular. While Shanghai's population growth rate has been the lowest in China, the growth of the industrial labour force has been large — increasing from 2.4 million in 1957 to 3 million in 1975. Labour productivity rose by over 5% per annum between 1966 and 1975.

Before 1949, Shanghai had little heavy industry. Now ship-building, machine tools, motor vehicles, electrical equipment and chemicals are all important industries, and Shanghai's steel industry has become the second largest in China. The textile industry — which has long been one of Shanghai's main industries — has been subject to stringent constraints on growth and pressures to diversify. Nevertheless production has increased, and the city now provides a third of China's total textile exports.

Over 80% of Shanghai's industrial products are sent to other parts of China, or are exported. Similarly 85% of its consumer goods leave the city. It is clear that post-1949 attempts to transform Shanghai from a basically 'consumer' city into a 'producer' city have dramatically succeeded.

With this background, Shanghai is obviously an ideal place for the foreign visitor to tour factories. CITS can arrange visits to a variety of heavy industry plants, including a steel mill, oil refinery, or a machine tool factory (particularly interesting is Shanghai Machine Tool Plant Number One which was one of the late Chairman Mao's favourites). Visits to one of the Shanghai watch factories, to the Shanghai brewery, or to one of the many textile mills are also to be recommended.

CITS also arranges trips to factories producing traditional arts and crafts. These always have small shops selling the goods made in the factory. The workshops of the Shanghai Jade and Ivory Carving Factory are frequently visited, and the Shanghai Carpet Factory nearby is another popular tour with foreign visitors. Most of the hand loom carpets made at the factory are for export, and some can be bought on the spot. Many of the carpet designs are traditional, but the factory will make woollen tapestries to order. Visitors are usually shown the weaving section, with workers expertly threading and trimming the wool on floor-to-ceiling looms, and also the clipping section, where the embossed carpet designs are created by skilful manipulation of electric shears.

Fuxing Park

This attractive park is situated in the south-central section of the city — take a left into Chongqing Road from Huaihai Middle Road and you will find the park further down on the left. The park was built in 1909 and has some notable features which make it outstanding among Shanghai's major parks. There are massive trees which provide excellent shade during the hot summer months. There is also a small zoo. In the early morning the park is full of activity with people of all ages jogging and practising *taiqiquan*. During the afternoons elderly people play cards and Chinese chess while women look after small children. Parks are always a good place to meet local people, and here you may encounter many of the younger Shanghainese anxious to practise their English. For those staying at the Jinjiang Hotel the park is just a short walk away.

Guilin Park

Located in the southwest suburbs, the park was built in 1933 in the grounds of Huang Jinrong's house. Huang Jinrong was one of Shanghai's most famous gangsters, or *liumang* as they are called in

Chinese. The park is built after the Suzhou style and is a very pleasant place to spend an afternoon.

Hongkou Park

Built in 1905 this park was once part of the Japanese section of the city. Today it houses the Lu Xun Memorial (see page 78). There are rowing boats for hire here but it is often difficult to get one since this is one of Shanghai's most popular parks. Occasionally lantern exhibitions are held in the park and in the autumn large crowds turn out to view the spectacular chrysanthemum display.

Huxinting Teahouse

At the entrance of the Yu Garden there is a small rectangular lake with the famous Huxinting Teahouse in the centre. The bridge of nine turnings (zigzagged, it is said, because evil spirits cannot go round corners) leads to the old five-sided teahouse pavilion. The building may well be familiar to visitors, since it was a symbol of Shanghai during the time of the foreign concessions, and frequently appeared on plates and souvenirs from the city. The teahouse is packed throughout the day with workers and retired people, who come to sip tea, talk, and watch the endless stream of passers-by in the surrounding streets of the Old Chinese City.

Jingan Temple

This Buddhist temple dates from the 19th century. A stone column, which is a copy of the Ashoka capital, stands in the middle of the road in front of it. Situated opposite the small much-used Jingan Park, and just off the busy Nanjing Road West, the temple today belies its name of the Temple of Serenity.

The temple's colourful past is probably more interesting than the present buildings, which have been considerably reduced and are not especially spectacular. Before 1949, it was one of the richest and most constantly used of Shanghai's many temples. It was run by the now almost legendary Abbot of Bubbling Well Road — a massive shaven-headed man, six foot four inches tall, who had a fabulously wealthy wife, seven concubines, and his own White Russian bodyguard.

Longhua Pagoda and Temple

This attractive eight-sided pagoda in the southwest of the city was first built in 274, and then rebuilt at the beginning of the Song Dynasty (960-1279). With seven storeys, the 120-foot high pagoda is a prominent landmark. As the only pagoda in the city of Shanghai, it was a popular tourist spot for foreigners during the first half of this century, and proved particularly fascinating since the building tilts slightly to one side. It is now again being included on some itineraries for foreign tourists.

The temple buildings, which date from the Qing Dynasty (1644-1911), cover a large area. There are four halls containing many statues of the Buddha and disciples, including one 10-foot high statue of the laughing Buddha.

The pleasant horticultural gardens nearby are full of attractive seasonal displays of potted plants — rhododendrons, orchids, freesias, azaleas — and miniature bonsai landscapes with rocks and flowers.

Lu Xun Museum, Tomb, and Former Residence

Lu Xun (1881-1936) a great man of letters, a thinker and revolutionary, is the most revered of the 20th-century Chinese writers. He was an early supporter of the peasants' cause, the need for universal education, and the 1911 Revolution, although he in fact never joined the Communist Party. He became associated with the budding literary revolution when, in 1918, he published his famous short story *A Madman's Diary*, a repudiation of Confucian culture and the first western-style story written in Chinese. While teaching at universities in Hangzhou, Amoy, Canton and Shanghai, he pro-

Huxinting Teahouse

duced poetry and essays, novels, such as his great masterpiece *The True Story of Ah Q*, and many translations of Russian, Japanese and German works. Sometimes referred to as 'the Chinese Gorki', Lu Xun's work throughout his life consistently denounced social injustices.

Lu Xun moved to Shanghai in 1927, where he lived until his death in 1936. He was prominent among the fifty or so intellectuals who first set up the League of Leftist Writers of China in Shanghai in 1930, and who adopted the programme which was to be the charter for the new revolutionary literature in China.

In 1956, Lu Xun's ashes were removed with great ceremony from the international cemetery in the western suburbs, to a tomb in the attractive Hongkou Park. In front of the tomb is a bronze statue of the writer. The six characters on the tomb — which say 'Lu Xun's tomb' — were inscribed by the late Chairman Mao. The two trees beside the tomb were planted by Chou En-lai and Lu Xun's widow.

Nearby, in the park, is a museum dedicated to the life and work of the writer. Although many of the exhibits are in Chinese, anyone interested in the history of this era will appreciate the wealth of old

Shoe factory

newspaper photographs, and others will enjoy the woodblock prints illustrating the first editions of Lu Xun's works. There are translations of his works, and of works written on him, as well as reconstructions of his study and bedroom.

During the last three and a half years of his life, Lu Xun lived in Shanyin Road just south of Hongkou Park. The red-brick house is now open to the public, with the rooms supposedly arranged in the way they were during Lu Xun's lifetime.

Old Chinese City

The Old Chinese City which is located to the west of Renmin Road and bordered by Zhonghua Road, is the oldest inhabited part of Shanghai. It was here in the 19th century that international missionary groups set up their first churches and communities. Today these churches no longer exist and neither do the tightly-packed, rat-infested slums which once predominated in the area. In the 1920s and '30s it was a place where few foreigners dared to wander. Today, though the streets have been cleaned up, they are still narrow and crowded, giving the Old Chinese City a special air that hints of past adventure and strange happenings.

Throughout the Old Chinese City there are restaurants and small markets selling fresh fruit and vegetables. In the northeast part is a bazaar selling traditional Chinese handicrafts such as lanterns, finely carved walking-sticks, jewelry and ceramics. Should you get tired of walking you can always rest in the beautiful old Huxingting Teahouse at the entrance of the Yu Garden (see page 92).

The Port

Shanghai is one of China's largest ports, with wharfs stretching 35 miles along the wide muddy Huangpu River. The great central waterway of China, the Yangtse River, is little more than ten miles north of the city, and not only links Shanghai with important cities of the interior — Nanjing (Nanking), Wuhan and Chongqing (Chungking) — but also connects Shanghai to the Yellow Sea.

It has been estimated that Shanghai now handles more than a third of China's seagoing freight, and extensive redevelopment plans will greatly increase the port's capacity. Already the volume of goods handled has risen from 42 million tons in 1972 to 72 million tons in 1978, and it is expected that the port will be able to handle 150 million tons by 1985. Containerization is being introduced, and cargo handling will be computerized. A modern seaway is being constructed to allow ships of up to 50,000 tons to enter the harbour.

It is difficult for foreign tourists to see much of the dock area, but the four-hour river trip down to the mouth of the Yangtse, on a large cruise boat which leaves from the wharf opposite the Peace Hotel, provides an opportunity for looking at Shanghai's port activities.

Renmin Park and Renmin Square

The concentration of shops in Nanjing Road is relieved by the greenery of Renmin (or People's) Park. Laid out on what used to be the British-run racecourse, the park is a pleasant 30-acre oasis of trees, pools and decorative rocks. A section of the old racetrack grandstand serves as a rostrum for big meetings, and the old Racing Club building now houses the Shanghai Municipal Library, which is said to contain 6.2 million volumes.

On the south side of the Park is the enormous Renmin Square. Laid out in 1951, the square is 150 yards long and several hundred yards wide. This wide open space is given much daily use by groups of schoolchildren practising gymnastics, and young people doing military training or learning to ride bicycles. It is also, of course, the setting for mass rallies and important parades.

Residential Areas

Since 1949, many of Shanghai's worst slum areas have been cleared, and modern apartment blocks have been built for the workers, often near the factories where they work. An interesting visit to one of these new residential areas can be arranged for groups of foreign visitors. The group is usually met by a representative of the neighbourhood who explains and answers questions about the area. The visitors will then be shown some of the neighbourhood's facilities — perhaps a school, kindergarten or clinic — and will probably be invited into one of the apartments to meet and talk with the family living there.

Shanghai Arts and Crafts Research Institute

Some of China's most skilled artisans in traditional crafts can be seen at work here. There are workers producing needlepoint landscapes and portraits in wool, silk embroidery pictures, stone carvings, lanterns, artificial flowers, papercuts, bamboo carvings and lacquer work. A fascinating demonstration in the art of modelling figurines out of dough is also often given to visitors.

The old mansion which houses the Institute is well worth visiting for itself. This unusually well-preserved European-style house, with its spacious lawns, conjures up some impression of the former grandeur of the French Concession area.

A shop at the entrance gates sells some of the items that are produced at the Institute.

Shanghai Art Exhibition Hall

This hall for temporary exhibitions is located in the centre of the city at the corner of Huangbei Road and Nanjing Road West. Any of the exhibitions held here would be worth seeing. In the last few years exhibitions have ranged from traditional Chinese paintings and wood blocks to photography and the work of local artists. Works from abroad have recently been shown to a wide and very appreciative audience.

Shanghai Industrial Exhibition Hall

This vast hall in Yan'an Road, built in 1955 very much in the same style as the Peking Exhibition Centre, was first known as the Palace of Sino-Soviet Friendship. With its tapering spire and cavernous interior, the style is strictly Soviet baroque.

figures, discovered recently less than a mile from the tumulus of the first Qin emperor, built between 247 and 211BC.

In the same room is a collection of attractive funerary pottery from the southern regions of China. Small clay figurines from the Han period (206BC-AD220) give a vivid picture of life at that time, with models of a watch-tower, a poultry-yard, a pigsty, the grand house of a wealthy man, and some charming figures of animals — ducks, dogs, horses, chickens.

The rooms devoted to pottery of the Tang period (619-907) has some particularly fine tomb figurines in the famous six-coloured Tang pottery — red, black, white, brown, green and yellow. There are well observed figures of women playing polo, elegant Tang Dynasty court ladies, each with their own personalities, an ox-cart, as well as the more familiar Tang figures of horses and camels.

Other pieces to look out for in the pottery collection include a series of richly-coloured porcelain headrests from the Song period (960-1279), together with a small collection of exquisite pale celadon pieces, some polychrome Yuan period wares (1279-1388) and examples of Ming blue and white dishes.

Paintings and Prints The top floor follows the development of painting in China, beginning with some drawings on pottery, and reproductions of mural paintings from tombs. The collection contains a wealth of paintings and prints from the Song, Yuan, Ming and Qing periods. There are many particularly fine paintings from the Tang and Song periods depicting scenes of everyday life, a fascinating record of the times. As many of the paintings are extremely delicate, and easily affected by light, they are usually only briefly on display, or are replaced by copies.

This floor also has an interesting collection of old implements used in painting and calligraphy — brushes, inkstands — and a replica of a scholar's study in the Yuan period (1279-1368).

Shanghai Natural History Museum

Located at 260 Yan'an Road just a couple of blocks southwest of the Peace Hotel, this is one of Shanghai's major museums. The museum was built in 1956 and has an extensive collection of ancient and modern exhibits. There are often specific exhibitions going on, some of which are interesting in a general way, but the museum still has a long way to go in organizing its collections. There are also small permanent collections on view. The museum is open 8.30 am – 10.30 am and 1.30 – 3.30 pm and at 10.00 am there is a film show. It is closed on Thursday and Saturday afternoons.

Site of the First National Congress of the Chinese Communist Party

At 76 Xingye Road, a small street near Fuxing Park, is a beautifully restored grey-brick house where, in July 1921, the Chinese Communist Party was officially born. It was here that 12 Communists, including Mao Tse-tung, held their First Party Congress. Although the house was owned by one of the members, the meeting was illegal under the laws of the French Concession. After meeting for three days, the Congress was betrayed and the members narrowly escaped to Nan Lake in Jiaxing, 70 miles south of the city. They rented a tourist boat, and resumed their meeting on the lake.

The room in Xingye Road where they met is arranged with 12 seats around a table set with tea bowls and ashtrays. In two adjoining rooms is an illustrated history of the Chinese Communist Party, with youthful pictures of Mao and other party founders, a copy of the first Chinese translation of Marx's *Communist Manifesto*, and an account of the lives of the 12 Congress members.

The display is now being reorganized in the light of the current re-evaluation of the early history of the Chinese Communist Party. Although the display is in Chinese, good English-speaking guides are available.

Temple lion

Sun Yat-sen Museum

Sun Yat-sen, the key figure in the 1911 Revolution against the Manchus, and the founder of the Guomindang — the Chinese Nationalist Party — is revered by all Chinese as the founder of modern China. Before his death in Peking in 1925 he lived for a short time in Shanghai, at Zhongqing Road South, near Fuxing Park. The house has been attractively restored and now contains a small museum with memorabilia of Dr Sun.

Temple of the Heavenly Mother

This temple is just north of Suzhou Creek on Henan Road North. The building was an imperial foundation and was thus free from municipal council rule. The remains of the temple include part of the forecourt, the main gate and a portion of the main courtyard. But most of the area originally covered by this temple is now occupied by a modern building. The original building reputedly served as the yamen of the Shanghai Daotai (Chief Magistrate) and possibly at one time it was a customs house before the setting up of the Chinese Imperial Maritime Customs. There is some doubt, though, whether the area was first a temple or a yamen.

Temple of the Jade Buddha

Temple of the Jade Buddha

This temple, famous for its two jade images of the Buddha, stands amidst the factories and urban sprawl of the northwest of the city. Now in active use, with over 20 Buddhist monks in attendance, the temple has recently been fully restored. The temple walls and the enormous gilded wooden statues have been richly repainted in magnificent colours.

The complex of temple buildings is comparatively new, built in 1911 and 1918, and is not in itself especially interesting, but there are some beautiful objects to look at. Most famous are the white jade images of the Buddha. At ground level there is a small graceful reclining Buddha, and, in a special hall reached by climbing up some very steep wooden stairs, there is the larger seated Buddha, with inlaid precious stones decorating the robes. This room also contains Ming editions of 7240 of the Buddhist sutras. Following the Buddhist custom, visitors have to remove their shoes before entering the room.

There are guides on hand who speak several different western languages, and for shoppers, a branch of the Shanghai Antiques and Curios Store has now been opened inside the temple.

Temple of the Town Gods

Every town used to possess a temple to the town gods, but this is one of the few now surviving. The temple, Chenghuang miao, is near the Yu Garden in the Old Chinese City, and is now being used as a warehouse. It had two statues — one of the patron saint of the city, Lao Zi, and another of a local hero General Huo Guang. The temple has still to become one of Shanghai's established tourist sights.

The Waterfront

A wide avenue curves along the west bank of the Huangpu River, dominated on one side by an imposing line of buildings in the grand European style which overlook the waterfront. This impressive avenue, now called Zhongshan Number One Road East, was the famous Bund, probably the best known of all streets in the East.

In the days of the foreign concessions, the Bund was the focal point of the city. It was both a hectic waterfront, with every conceivable kind of boat from sampans to large cargo vessels anchoring there, and, at the same time, one of Shanghai's main streets. Contemporary accounts describe vividly the continuous noisy street activity, as beggars, hawkers, and black marketeers mingled with coolies, seamen, and the businessmen from the great trading houses and banks that lined the street. The road was constantly jammed with trucks, mule carts, trams, motor cars and rickshaws.

Today Shanghai's main wharfs are further down the river, the frenetic street life has gone, and the Bund has acquired a different mood. Trolleybuses, bicycles and taxis drive fast along the broad avenue, while pedestrians stroll by the river or sit in the small Huangpu Park, or, early in the morning, do their *taijiquan* exercises. The buildings now house state corporations and government offices — such as the Foreign Trade Corporations, the Textile Bureau, the River Board Office, and the Trade Union Headquarters. Only the former Cathay Hotel remains as a hotel — the Peace Hotel — and the Tudor-style building with its tall clock tower is still the Customs House, although now free of its former foreign controllers. But a walk along the Bund past the solid facades is still evocative of Shanghai's past. Starting at the Waibaidu Bridge (formerly Garden Bridge), you pass the gates to the former British Consulate and the buildings which at one time housed the offices of Glen Line, Jardine Matheson, the Bank of Indo-China, the Yokohama Specie Bank. In the buildings to the south of Nanjing Road were the *North China Daily News* offices, the Chartered Bank, the British-built Lyceum Theatre, the Shanghai Club, now the Dongfeng Hotel, and the Hongkong and Shanghai Bank, now the offices of the Shanghai Municipal Party Committee and the Municipal People's Government.

Workers' Cultural Palace (formerly Dashijie)

This cultural palace, one of many in Shanghai, was formerly Dashijie, the Great World, a famous entertainment and gambling centre in the 1920s. It is located on Xizang Middle Road at the junction with Yan'an Middle Road. The seven-storey building contains a surprising range of facilities. There are two theatres used for a wide variety of cultural shows and for films. There are also large exhibition areas, a sports hall, chess facilities, and numerous rooms devoted to cultural activities — everything from singing and dancing to arts and crafts, music and drama. Occasionally it is difficult for foreigners to get into this cultural palace but if you do get the chance it is certainly worth the trip.

Xujiahui Cathedral

Located in Xujiahui district in the southwest of the city, the Cathedral of St. Ignatius was built in 1906. Its bell tower is 160 feet high and the spires which were damaged during the Cultural Revolution are now being repaired. This is Shanghai's largest Catholic church and has room for 2500 people at any given service though many more come and have to stand (see page 49).

During the Taiping Rebellion in the middle of the 19th century the area of Xujiahui was used as the headquarters of the rebels. It was once also the site of St. Ignatius College and Seminary. The foundation of the complex was laid out in 1848. By 1920 the complex consisted of an orphange, industrial school, a library and the Xujiahui printing press and church.

Xijiao Park

The Xijiao lies in the far west of the city, quite near Hongqiao Airport and not far from Shanghai Zoo. It is a delightful little park where few foreigners ever venture. There are a number of small lakes and pavilions where it is pleasant just to sit and escape from the din and pollution of the city. There is also a roller-skating rink for those who feel they have to exercise everywhere they go.

Bargemen, Suzhou Creek

Sailors on the Bund

Yu Garden

The Yu Garden, in the north of the Old Chinese City, is the only fully-restored classical Chinese garden in Shanghai, and is similar to many of the famous gardens of Suzhou. Work on laying out the garden, which was created for a Ming Dynasty official, was begun in 1537.

For the Chinese, gardens were a microcosm in which the skilful gardener — who had to combine the qualities of a painter, poet, architect, and landscape gardener — could construct his own world using minerals, plants and animals, in a limited space. Although the Yu Garden occupies less than five acres, it seems far larger when walking round. The garden demonstrates perfectly the sophisticated art of combining several different elements to create a world in miniature — ingeniously mingling pavilions and corridors, small hills and carefully selected and placed rocks, lotus ponds with goldfish swimming in them, bridges, winding paths, trees and shrubs.

There are many details in the garden to look out for. Each section is divided up by white curving walls that are topped by the undulating body of a dragon. The walls end with splendidly carved dragon heads. There are fine examples of the type of carved bricks found in Suzhou's gardens — earthenware pictures of animals, flowers, or scenes illustrating legends. Many shapes and designs of ornamental windows — square, round, rectangular and polygonal — can be seen, with highly complicated lattice patterns.

The garden contains over 30 pavilions, and a labyrinth of stairs, corridors and pathways. The highest point is the Rockery Hill, an artificial mountain made of rocks said to have been brought from thousands of miles away, and cemented together with a kind of rice glue. An ancient-looking gingko tree is reputedly over 400 years old, and a magnolia tree and a wisteria plant which still flowers every Spring, are both said to have been in the garden for more than 200 years. A large curiously shaped rock, standing in front of the Hall of Jade Magnificence, is known as the Exquisite Jade Rock and was, it is claimed, found under water during the Song Dynasty (960-1279). During the Taiping Rebellion some citizens of Shanghai, known as the 'Society of Little Swords', joined this peasant uprising against the Qing Dynasty, organising a rebellion from within the walls of the city in 1853. They used the Hall of Heralding Spring as their head-quarters, and managed to inflict considerable damage on foreign and imperial troops before they were finally defeated in 1854. The Hall now contains a small museum of the uprising.

The Inner Garden, which at one time belonged to the Temple of the Town Gods, was recently restored, and is now open to the public. And, on a more commercial note, the Yu Garden now also contains a branch of the Antiques and Curios Store, open specially for foreign tourists.

The garden is highly popular with the people of Shanghai — particularly the young who come here to photograph each other — and can sometimes be uncomfortably crowded.

Zhangfeng Park

Zhangfeng Park is one of Shanghai's new parks. Built in 1959 it covers an area of over 34 hectares and is located next to East China Normal University. Its chief attraction is the small lake in the middle of the park where you can go boating and escape the noise of the city. There is a small restaurant at the side of the lake where you can have a meal or just sit quietly and drink tea.

The Zoo

The Zoo is located in the western suburbs of the city on Hongqiao Road. Before 1949 it was the city's main golf course but was converted into a zoo in 1954 with an area of 70 hectares. There are some 300 species of animals and birds to see here, both native to China and foreign. A great draw for foreigners is, of course, the Giant Panda.

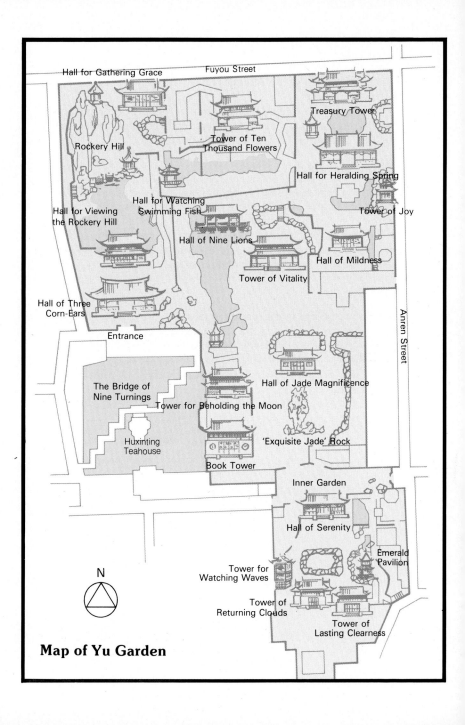

Hall for Gathering Grace   Fuyou Street

Treasury Tower

Tower of Ten
Thousand Flowers

Rockery Hill

Hall for Heralding Spring

Hall for Viewing
the Rockery Hill

Hall for Watching
Swimming Fish

Tower of Joy

Hall of Nine Lions

Hall of Mildness

Tower of Vitality

Hall of Three
Corn-Ears

Entrance

Anren Street

The Bridge of
Nine Turnings

Hall of Jade Magnificence

Tower for Beholding the Moon

Huxinting
Teahouse

'Exquisite Jade' Rock

Book Tower

Inner Garden

Hall of Serenity

Emerald
Pavilion

Tower for
Watching Waves

Tower of
Returning Clouds

Tower of
Lasting Clearness

N

Map of Yu Garden

Yu Garden

Sights outside Shanghai

Those staying several weeks in Shanghai who have seen the major sights of the city might find a visit to one of the outlying counties a worthwhile experience. The journey would offer a chance to look at the countryside and some small towns not usually visited by foreigners, and there are also some interesting temples and pagodas to see. Transport by public bus will take 1-3 hours depending on the traffic and the distance you are going.

Communes

Foreign tourists have a chance to visit communes in many of the recently opened areas of China, but a visit to a commune in one of the ten counties of the Municipality of Shanghai is particularly interesting, for the communes here are amongst the most successful in China.

One reason for Shanghai's great economic success over the past 30 years has in fact been the considerable support given by its 199 communes. The Municipality of Shanghai now has a higher productivity per area of land than anywhere else in China. The communes have three crops a year — one of winter wheat and two of rice — and large quantities of pork and vegetables are produced. Shanghai's agriculture is now highly mechanized — almost the entire region is irrigated by electric pump, and 90% of the land is ploughed by machine.

A commune visit may include a 'briefing' session, when a leading member will talk about the commune and answer questions. Visitors will perhaps tour a school, a commune factory, a hospital, clinic, or some agricultural buildings, and may be invited into a peasant's home to talk with the family that lives there. Some communes can also provide lunch for groups of foreign visitors.

Fahua Pagoda

The Fahua Pagoda is in the town of Jiading, on the south bank of the Lianqi, some 12 miles northwest of Shanghai. This Buddhist pagoda was built during the Southern Song (1205-1207). During the reign of Wang Li in 1608 the building was repaired but during the Qing Dynasty (1644-1911) the pagoda fell into serious disrepair and it was not until 1919 that the structure was rebuilt again using concrete and iron. The pagoda is not on the usual tour itineraries but if you have a chance to go then it is worth while. Take the bus from the Northern Bus Station on Gonghexin Road at the corner of Zhongshan Road North.

Guyi Garden

Guyi Garden is in Nanxiang, a town in Jiading County, northwest of the urban centre of Shanghai. It was first laid out in the Ming Dynasty (1522-1567), in the region of Jiajing, and later rebuilt during the Qianlong period (1736-1796). It has been renovated and extended since 1949, and now covers 16 acres. The garden still retains features of traditional Chinese gardens — pavilions, lakes, corridors, winding paths and bridges — and it has its own version of the famous marble boat in Peking's Summer Palace. Known as the 'untied boat', this is a small pavilion in the shape of a boat, built on a stone base in one of the garden's lakes. Take the bus for Jiading from the Northern Bus Station on Gonghexin Road at the corner of Zhongshan Road North.

Huayan Pagoda

Huayan, also called Songwen Pagoda, is to be found in the northeast of the town of Songwen in Jinshan County, southwest of Shanghai. In the Yuan Dynasty (1271-1368) the pagoda began life as a Buddhist monastery where the monks wrote the Huayan classics in 81 volumes. The money received from the sales helped to build the pagoda. The pagoda took four years to build and was completed in the early Ming Dynasty in 1380. It is a brick and wooden structure which, if you are travelling down the Huangpu River, you can see towering over the south bank. The pagoda is worth looking at since it remains one of the best examples of the kind of construction work done during the Ming Dynasty and it is almost complete. Take the bus for Jinshan from the Western Bus Station on Caoxi Road North at the corner of Pu Road West.

Jiading Confucian Temple

Located on Nanda Street in the town of Jiading in Jiading County, about 12 miles northwest of Shanghai, the temple was begun in 1218 during the Southern Song Dynasty and then restructured between 1241-1252. From the Yuan Dynasty through to the Qing Dynasty the temple was gradually extended to become one of the best temples in the Jiangnan region. In 1958 the temple was restored and now there is a small library with a cultural relics section which make up the County Library. Take the bus to Jiading from the Northern Bus Station on Gonghexin Road at the corner of Zhongshan North Road.

Songjiang

Songjiang is a small town 12 miles southeast of Shanghai, on the railway line to Hangzhou. It was founded under the Sui (589-618), and was well known at that time for a delicate fish known as a Song Perch or Song lu.

The Pagoda of Xingshengjiao Temple This nine-storey pagoda, often known as the Square Pagoda, stands in the southeast of the town. It was built in the 11th century, in the Song Dynasty. The pagoda is architecturally particularly interesting since, although it was restored during the Ming and Qing periods, much of the original 11th-century brick and wood structure remains, with large wooden square blocks supporting the beams.

Songjiang Screen Wall Also worth visiting in the town is a large screen wall erected in 1370 during the reign of the Ming Emperor Hongwu. The wall is decorated with a massive brick bas-relief, 20 feet long and 15 feet high, of an imposing legendary beast — the 'monster of avarice' — which apparently tried to eat everything on earth, and finally drowned by rushing into the sea to swallow up the rising sun. The monster is surrounded by intricate patterns of flowers, trees, rocks, and animals.

Take the bus from the Western Bus Station on Caoxi Road North at the corner of Pu Road West.

Taiping Tianguo Grave of Revolutionary Martyrs

This monument is located in the northeast of Gaoqiao, a town in Shanghai's Chuansha County. In 1862 the rebels of the Taiping Army invaded the surrounding counties and quickly established their headquarters in the area. It was here that the rebels were confronted and eventually beaten by invading foreign forces, and a great number of rebels were killed. The civil cultural authorities marked this site as a historical grave in 1954. Take the bus for Chuansha from Tanqiao Bus Station on Pudong South Road at the corner of Pujian Road.

Qinglong Pagoda

The Qinglong Pagoda is also known as the Jinyu Monastery Temple Pagoda. It lies just over half a mile from old Qingpu town near the ancient town of Qinglong in Qingpu County some 14 miles due west from Shanghai. During the Tang Dynasty (618-907) and the Song Dynasty (960-1127) the town of Qingpu was a flourishing market and port where merchants gathered to carry on local and foreign trade. It was so busy that the town became known as Little

Hangzhou and in the surrounding area shrines and temples proliferated. In 743 Baode Temple was built and the Qinglong Pagoda was added in 821. At the same time the temple was renamed Longfu. The last major restructuring of the pagoda was during the Northern Song between 1041-48 when the temple again changed its name to Jinyu Monastery Temple. The original structure was of brick and wood but today it is all brick and in the style of the Song Dynasty. The area around Qingpu fell into disuse as a market and business centre, and the temples and shrines gradually disappeared leaving just one pagoda as a witness to the area's rich history. Take the bus for Qingpu from the Western Bus Station on Caoxi Road North at the corner of Pu Road West.

Qushui Garden

Originally called the Ling Garden it is to be found in the northeast corner of Qingpu, a town in Qingpu County, facing Yingpu. The garden was completed in 1745 during the reign of the famous emperor, Qianlong. In the garden there are several tranquil scenic spots and in the northern part a hill from which not only the garden but also the surrounding hills can be viewed. In 1927 the garden was redeveloped and changed its name to Zhongshan Garden, but basically the style and features remain those of the old garden. Take the bus for Qingpu from the Western Bus Station on Caoxi Road North at the corner of Pu Road West.

Zhenru Temple

The Zhenru Temple is to be found on Nanda Street in Zhenru, a town in Jiading County northwest of Shanghai. The temple was built in 1320. Most of the present buildings date from the Yuan Dynasty but there have been a few additions. When the temple was restored in 1963 it was discovered that many of the original craftsmen working on the temple had written their names and their positions on the wooden parts of the structure. The writing is now an important source material for those studying calligraphy. The building as a whole is a fine example of 14th-century architecture which provides much information on old construction techniques. Take the bus for Jiading from the Northern Bus Station on Gonghexin Road at the corner of Zhongshan Road North.

Recommended Reading

Much of the most fascinating reading on Shanghai covers the period of the foreign concessions before 1949. Most of the books are out of print but are worth looking for in libraries or secondhand bookshops. G. Miller's *Shanghai, the Paradise of Adventurers* (Orsay 1937), written under a pseudonym by an American diplomat, was one of the best-known books on pre-1949 Shanghai. *Shanghai: A Handbook for Travellers and Residents* (Kelly and Walsh 1920), listing 'the chief objects of interest in and around the foreign settlements and native city', is an interesting period guidebook by the Reverend Charles Darwent.

A highly readable account of the city during the time of the Communist takeover is Noel Barber's *The Fall of Shanghai: The Communist Takeover in 1949* (Macmillan 1979) which draws extensively on interviews with people who lived through the period. Lawrence Earl's *Yangtze Incident* (Harrap 1950) focuses on the adventures of the British frigate HMS *Amethyst* during the takeover.

A powerful description of conditions in Shanghai during the '30s is to be found in André Malraux's *Man's Estate* (Penguin 1961), first published in French in 1933 as *La Condition Humaine*. In the same year the Chinese writer Mao Dun also published his great novel set in Shanghai, *Midnight* (Peking Foreign Languages Press, 2nd edition 1979), which centres on a Chinese industrial capitalist in Shanghai.

For a history of Shanghai from its earliest days there is *Yellow Creek: the Story of Shanghai* by J.V. Davidson-Houston (Putnam 1962). The period of the Cultural Revolution is covered in Neil Hunter's interesting *Shanghai Journal: an Eyewitness Account of the Cultural Revolution* (Praeger 1969). Shanghai is one of the cities treated in Ross Terrill's *Flowers on an Iron Tree: Five Cities of China* (Little, Brown 1975), which offers a graphic description of Shanghai at the time of Terrill's visit there in 1973. The most recent interesting book on Shanghai's past is Pan Ling's *In Search of Old Shanghai* (Joint Publishing Company, Hong Kong, 1982). The book is short and is very useful as a companion to a guide of Shanghai.

Useful Addresses

Airlines and Airport

CAAC
789 Yan'an Middle Road
Reservations International tel. 532255
            Domestic tel. 535953
Cargo   International tel. 531640
            Domestic tel. 535363
            Delivery tel. 535632
中国民航   延安中路 789 号

Cathay Pacific Airlines
Jinjiang Hotel, Room 123, tel. 534242
国泰航空公司   锦江饭店 123 号房间

Japan Airlines
1202 Huaihai Middle Road,
Huaihai Apartments, Room 102, tel. 378467
日本航空公司   淮海中路 1202 淮海公寓

Pan American World Airways
Jingan Guesthouse, Room 103, tel. 563050
Airport Office, tel. 531935/536530 ext. 364
泛美航空公司   静安宾馆 103 号房间

Airport
Hongqiao Airport Inquiries, tel. 537664
虹桥飞机场

Antiques and Curios

Antiques and Curios Store
218-226 Guangdong Road, tel. 212864
文物商店   广东路 218-226 号
      Jade Buddha Temple Branch
      170 Anyuan Road, tel. 535843
      玉佛寺分店   安远路 170 号
      Yu Garden Branch
      Yu Garden, tel. 289109
      豫园分店   豫园

Arts and Crafts Store
190 Nanjing Road West, tel. 537238
上海工艺美术服务部   南京西路 190 号

Banks

Bank of China
23 Zhongshan Number One Road East,
tel. 217466
中国银行   中山东一路 23 号

Chartered Bank
185 Yuanmingyuan Road, tel. 218253
渣打银行   圆明园路 185 号

Hong Kong and Shanghai Banking Corporation
185 Yuanmingyuan Road, tel. 216030
香港汇丰银行   圆明园路 185 号

Banque Nationale de Paris
Peace Hotel, 5th Floor, Room 509, tel. 211244
法国国家巴黎银行   和平饭店五楼 509 室

Bookshops

China Classics Bookstore
424 Fuzhou Road, tel. 223453/224984
古籍书店   福州路 424 号

Shanghai Bookstore
401-411 Fuzhou Road, tel. 282894
上海书店   福州路 401-411 号

Shanghai Foreign Languages Bookshop
390 Fuzhou Road, tel. 224109
外文书店   福州路 390 号

Shanghai Science and Technology Bookshop
221 Henan Middle Road, tel. 21766
上海科技书店   河南中路 221 号

Xinhua Bookstore
345 Nanjing Road East, tel. 222964
新华书店   南京东路 345 号

Churches and Mosques

Catholic Church
Xujiahui
徐家汇

International Church
Hengshan Road
衡山路

Kunshan Protestant Church
Kunshan Road
昆山路

Shanghai Mosque
Fuyou Road
福佑路

Zhabei Church
Baotong Road
宝通路

Cinemas

Da Shanghai Cinema
500 Xizang Middle Road, tel. 293322
大上海电影院　西藏中路500号

Daguangming Cinema
216 Nanjing Road West, tel. 532223
大光明电影院　南京西路216号

Guotai Cinema
870 Huaihai Middle Road, tel. 373757
国泰电影院　淮海中路870号

Huaihai Cinema
555 Huaihai Middle Road, tel. 288467
淮海电影院　淮海中路555号

Huguang Cinema
725 Yan'an Road East, tel. 285855
沪光电影院　延安东路725号

Pingan Cinema
1193 Nanjing Road West, tel. 538484
平安电影院　南京西路1193号

Xinhua Cinema
742 Nanjing Road West, tel. 538050
新华电影院　南京西路742号

Clubs

International Club
65 Yan'an Road West, tel. 538455/537040
国际俱乐部　延安西路65号

Jinjiang Club
58 Maoming Road, tel. 375334
锦江俱乐部　茂名路58号

Consulates

France
1431 Huaihai Middle Road, tel. 377414
法国领事馆　淮海中路1431号

Japan
1517 Huaihai Middle Road, tel. 379025
日本领事馆　淮海中路1517号

The Polish People's Republic
618 Jianguo Road West, tel. 370952/376683
波兰领事馆　建国西路618号

The United States of America
1496 Huaihai Middle Road, tel. 379880
美国领事馆　淮海中路1496号

West Germany
151 Yongfu Road, tel. 378812
西德领事馆　永福路151号

Department Stores and Specialist Shops

Friendship Store
33 Zhongshan Number One Road East,
tel. 219698
友谊商店　中山东一路33号
　　　　Antiques and Curios Branch
　　　　694 Nanjing Road West, tel. 538092
　　　文物商店　南京西路694号

Laojiefu Silk Shop
257 Nanjing Road East, tel. 219292
老介福呢绒绸缎商店　南京东路257号

Number One Department Store
830 Nanjing Road East, tel. 223344
第一百货商店　南京东路830号

Number One Food Store
720 Nanjing Road East, tel. 222777
第一食品商店　南京东路720号

Number Ten Department Store
635 Nanjing Road East, tel. 224466
第十百货商店 南京东路635号

Number Two Department Store
889-909 Huaihai Middle Road, tel. 374414
第二百货商店 淮海中路889-909号

Overseas Chinese Department Store
627 Nanjing Road East, tel. 225424
华侨商店 南京东路627号

Shanghai Clothing Store
690 Nanjing Road East, tel. 225445
上海服装商店 南京东路690号

Shanghai Women's Store
449-471 Huaihai Middle Road, tel. 285999
上海市妇女用品商店 淮海中路449-471号

Xiangyang Children's Shop
993 Nanjing Road West, tel. 537588
向阳儿童用品商店 南京西路993号

Hospitals

East China Hospital (Huadong Yiyuan)
257 Yan'an Road West, tel. 523125
华东医院 延安西路257号

Shanghai Number One Hospital
190 Suzhou Road North, tel. 240100
上海第一人民医院 苏州北路190号

Libraries

Shanghai Library
325 Nanjing Road West, tel. 562176
上海图书馆 南京西路325号

Museums

Shanghai Museum
16 Henan Road South, tel. 280160
上海博物馆 河南路16号

Shanghai Museum of Natural Science
260 Yan'an Road East, tel. 213548
上海自然博物馆 延安东路260号

Parks

Fuxing Park
105 Yandang Road, tel. 283296
复兴公园 雁荡路105号

Guilin Park
1 Guilin Road, tel. 380042
桂林公园 桂林路1号

Hongkou Park
146 Dongjiangwang Road, tel. 661187
虹口公园 东江湾路146号

Huangpu Park
18 Zhongshan Number One Road East,
tel. 214619
黄浦公园 中山东一路18号

Photography Shops

Guanlong Photographic Supplies Shop
180 Nanjing Road East, tel. 210883
冠尤照相材料商店 南京东路江西路180号

Hongyi Photographic Supply Shop
540 Huaihai Middle Road, tel. 283897
红艺照相材料商店 淮海中路540号

People's Photography Shop
831 Huaihai Middle Road, tel. 372387
人民照相馆 淮海中路831号

Seagull Photographic Supplies Shop
473 Nanjing Road East, tel. 221004
海鸥照相材料商店 南京东路473号

Post and Telecommunications

Shanghai Central Post Office
359 Tiantong Road
上海市邮政局 天潼路359号

Shanghai Telegraph Office
34 Nanjing Road East, tel. 211130
上海市电报局 南京东路34号

Police

Public Security Bureau, Foreigners Section
Hankou Road, tel. 215380
公安局外事科　汉口路

Theatres

Chanjiang Theatre
21 Huanghe Road, tel. 539531
长江剧场　黄河路21号

People's Theatre
663 Jiujiang Road, tel. 224473
人民大舞台　九江路663号

Shanghai Arts Theatre
57 Maoming Road, tel. 565544
上海艺术剧场　茂名南路57号

Shanghai Music Hall
523 Yan'an Road East, tel. 281714
上海音乐厅　延安东路523号

Worker's Theatre
701 Fuzhou Road, tel. 226270
劳动剧场　福州路701号

Trade

China Council for the Promotion of International Trade
27 Zhongshan Number One Road East, tel. 210722/3
中国国际贸易促进委员会　中山东一路27号

Shanghai Advertising Corporation
97 Yuanmingyuan Road, tel. 212999/214803
上海广告公司　圆明园路97号

Shanghai Branch of the Chinese Customs
13 Zhongshan Number One Road East, tel. 215529
中华人民共和国上海海关　中山东一路13号

Shanghai Culture and Art Management
709 Julu Road, tel. 378920
上海文艺术经理公司　巨鹿路709号

Travel

China International Travel Service (CITS)
66 Nanjing Road East, tel. 217200/214960
中国国际旅行社　南京东路66号

Shanghai Car Rentals
Automobiles, tel. 564444
Mini-buses, tel. 564444
出租汽车

Shanghai Friendship Taxi Company
40 Changle Road, tel. 536363
上海友谊汽车服务公司　长乐路40号

Shanghai Port Terminal
1 Taiping Road and Daming Road East, tel. 454320/452529
上海港国际客运站　东大名路太平路1号

Shanghai Railway Station
tel. 244020
上海火车站

Shanghai Train Information
tel. 242299
上海火车通知

Universities

Foreign Languages Institute
119 Xitiyuhui Road, tel. 660231
上海外国语学院　西体育会路119号

Fudan University
220 Handan Road, tel. 481240
复旦大学　邯郸路220号

Huadong (East China) Normal University
3663 Zhongshan Road North, tel. 548461
华东师范大学　中山北路3663号

Jiaotong University
1954 Huashan Road, tel. 370147
交通大学　华山路1954号

Shanghai First Medical College
138 Yixueyuan Road, tel. 375490
上海第一医学院　医学院路138号

Shanghai Music College
20 Fenyang Road, tel. 370137/370219
上海音乐学院　汾阳路 20 号

Tongji University
1239 Siping Road, tel. 455290
同济大学　四平路 1239 号

Index

A

B

C

S

T